JUST PROBLEMS

A Supplemental Symbolic Logic Workbook

JUST PROBLEMS

A Supplemental Symbolic Logic Workbook

E. R. Klein
Flagler College

WADSWORTH

THOMSON LEARNING

Australia • Canada • Mexico • Singapore • Spain • United Kingdom • United States

For permission to use material from this text,
contact us by **Web**: http://www.thomsonrights.com
Fax: 1-800-730-2215 **Phone:** 1-800-730-2214

ISBN 0-534-56101-2

For more information, contact
Wadsworth/Thomson Learning
10 Davis Drive
Belmont, CA 94002-3098
USA

For more information about our products, contact us
Thomson Learning Academic Resource Center
1-800-423-0563
http://www.wadsworth.com

International Headquarters
Thomson Learning
International Division
290 Harbor Drive, 2nd Floor
Stamford, CT 06902-7477
USA

UK/Europe/Middle East/South Africa
Thomson Learning
Berkshire House
168-173 High Holborn
London WC1V 7AA
United Kingdom

Asia
Thomson Learning
60 Albert Complex, #15-01
Singapore 189969

Canada
Nelson Thomson Learning
1120 Birchmount Road
Toronto, Ontario M1K 5G4
Canada

CONTENTS

Preface and Acknowledgments, pp.1-2.

     Chapter One: Tautologies, Contradictions and Contingencies, pp. 3-6.

     Chapter Two: Logical Equivalence, pp. 7-9.

     Chapter Three: Testing for Validity/Invalidity (Long Truth-Table Method), pp. 10-16.

     Chapter Four: Testing for Validity/Invalidity (Short Truth-Table Method), pp. 17-27.

     Chapter Five: Rules of Inference Part I, The "Eight Rules" (Partially Completed), pp. 28-33.

     Chapter Six: Rules of Inference Part II, The "Eight Rules", pp. 34-43.

     Chapter Seven: Rules of Replacement Part I, "Equivalencies" (Partially Completed), pp. 44-50.

     Chapter Eight: Rules of Replacement Part II, "Equivalencies", pp. 51-63.

     Chapter Nine: Conditional Proofs, pp. 64-68.

     Chapter Ten: Indirect Proofs, pp. 69-73.

     Chapter Eleven: Conditional Proofs and/or Indirect Proofs, pp. 74-81.

     Chapter Twelve: Proofs Using UI and EG, pp. 82-84.

     Chapter Thirteen: Proofs Using EI and UG, pp. 85-93.

     Chapter Fourteen: More Difficult Proofs Using All Quantification Rules, pp. 94-101.

     Chapter Fifteen: Proofs Using Relations, pp. 102-108.

     Chapter Sixteen: Flow-Charting, pp. 115.

   Key to Symbols and Terminology, pp. 116.

   Bibliography and Permissions, pp. 117-118.

   Appendix, pp. 119-121.

CONTENTS

Preface

Just Problems is a teaching tool for students and professors of symbolic logic. It's primary intent is to provide additional exercises and problem sets under each of the traditional symbolic logic categories. Since it is unfeasible to expect that any single text can both adequately teach all of the different areas of symbolic logic as well as provide ample and varied exercises and problems, *Just Problems* seems to be just the text the market needs. *Just Problems* is a cost-effective solution to the perennial problem of running out of assignments. Professors will be able to provide their students with additional problems and exercises (or students can take this initiative upon themselves) without resorting to the strenuous act of inventing their own problem sets, the all too tedious (and possibly illegal) activity of having to copy pages from additional texts, or the difficult and often expensive act of acquiring permissions from publishers.

In addition, *Just Problems* acts as an historical record of the various logic texts that have gone out of print. In today's fast paced market if a text is not immediately profitable it will go out of print long before its time. Given the enormous competition amongst symbolic logic texts, all too often fine texts—with interesting examples—lose market share to the most prestigious and powerful authors and presses. *Just Problems* not only attempts to save some of this hard work, it attempts to preserve problem sets from texts that have other historical and cultural value. Because the word problems from logic texts often reflect the political and social interests and concerns of the times, through word problems from, for example, Dr. Robert Neidorf's *Deductive Forms: An Elementary Logic*, 1967, one can see the way our culture has changed and grown. (Special thanks need to be given her to Mrs. Neidorf for her gracious permission to reprint her late husband's work.)

With the above in mind, in most cases I maintained a commitment to the original text with respect to both the form and content during reprinting. However, due to concerns of easy reading and consistency (as well as certain aesthetic considerations), there are times when I altered the form of the problem or exercise to better fit the layout of *Just Problems*. Content was altered only when I needed to change the author's wording in order to fit the truncated context. In addition I added a few of my own problems, examples and theory questions where I believed it was necessary.

The major feature of *Just Problems* is, simply, that it is a text containing just problems. Therefore, it does not directly compete with any specific logic text on the market, for its primary purpose is to be used as a supplementary text. As such it is designed to be used in conjunction with any and all logic texts (old or new) that are the personal favorites of students and faculty. Given, however, the variety of both symbolic notations and procedural terminology, I have provided a key in the back of the book for use in making the appropriate equivalent interpretations. (See **Key to Symbols and Terminology** preceding **Chapter Sixteen**.)

The workbook is divided into sixteen sections mimicking the outline of most contemporary symbolic logic texts. Professors or students can easily refer to any of the sections for which they may want to acquire additional examples or problems—the sections parallel traditional lessons. In addition, I have left space for students to work directly in the book if they choose to—which will allow them to keep their more expensive text of their choice free of any unnecessary markings. (The **Appendix**, at the very end of the workbook, is added to give the student a template for use in making truth tables which may be halpful for the exercises in **Chapter One, Chapter Two** and **Chapter Three.**

I would like to give thanks to all of the people who helped me with this project including Ms. Cynthia Barrncotto, Mrs. Margaret Draskovich , Ms. Peggy Dyess, Ms. Grace Engelstadeter, Mr. Michael Gallen, Mr. Brian Nesselrode, Ms. Catherine Norwood who patiently helped me to research and acquire out of print texts; Mr. Terry Bennett who helped with the compiling of the appropriate pages of text; Ms. Donna Langford for her help with the laser printer; Ms. Valerie Wishneski and Ms. Christina Wilson, for their technical assistance with word processing; as well as the administration of Flagler College—President Proctor, Vice President Abare, Dean Miller, and the Chair of my department Michael Sherman for their continued support of my faculty development

Special thanks go to my parents—Ron and Lil Klein, my fiancee Mr. Timothy Kotsis, and my most recent group of logic students. Spring semester 2000 at Flagler hosted the most wonderful and patient group of students including: Ms. Chelsey Cole, Mr. Jody Cone, Mr. Deke Gould, Ms. Caroline Kehl, Ms. Sarah Means, Mr. Christopher Mello, Mr. Anthony Santoloci, and Mr. Joseph Sherno, all of whom showed patience with *Just Problems* during its first trial run. In addition, I would like to thank everyone at Wadsworth, especially Ms. Kara Kindstrom.

Finally, let me give extra special thanks to Ms. Erin-Elizabeth Dolan, Ms. Cheryl Fitzgerald, and Mr. Nathan Vonderheid who not only participated in the Spring Semester while *Just Problems* was developed, but helped me with additional compilation and review during the summer of 2000.

Chapter One

Tautologies, Contradictions and Contingencies*

A. Use truth tables to determine whether the compounds in each pair below would be true under the same truth conditions for the variables "p" and "q." (Churchill, p.243)

    1. p ⊃ q and ~q ⊃ ~p
    2. p ≡ q and (p ⊃ q) & (q ⊃ p)
    3. p ⊃ q and ~p V q
    4. q ⊃ p and q V ~p
    5. p ≡ q and ~q ≡ ~p
    6. ~(p ⊃ q) and p V ~q
    7. ~(~p V ~q) and p V q
    8. ~(~p & ~q) and p & q
    9. ~(p & q) and ~p V ~q
    10. ~(p V q) and ~p & ~q

B. Determine whether the following are tautologies, contradictions, or neither (show your truth-tables) (Gustason, p.43):

    1. A v (~A & A)
    2. ~ (A&B) v A
    3. (A & ~B) v ~[~(B & C) & (C & A)]
    4. ~[(A v B) & C] v ~(D & B)
    5. (A & ~B) & [~A v (B & A)]

C. Construct a truth table for each of the statement forms below to determine whether a statement of that form is a tautology, contradiction, or a contingent statement. (Halverson, pp.176-177).

    1. (p V q) & p
    2. [(p ⊃ q) & p] ⊃ q
    3. [(p ⊃ q) & ~q] & p
    4. (p & ~q) ⊃ ~(p ⊃ q)
    5. (p ≡ q) & q
    6. p ⊃ ~(p V q)
    7. p ≡ ~q
    8. (p V q) ≡ r
    9. (p V q) ⊃ (~p ⊃ q)

---

* See the **Appendix** for a helpful template for use in doing the below exercises.

10. [p & (~p V q)] ⊃ q

D. Which of the following are tautologous, which contradictory, and which contingent? (McKay, p.77)

1. p & q
2. p V (~p & q)
3. p V ~p
4. ~p & (p & q)
5. (p V q) & ~(p & q)
6. (p & q) & ~(p V q)
7. [p & (q V ~p)] & ~p
8. (p & r) & ~q
9. (p V ~p) V q
10. (p V ~p) & q
11. (p V ~p) & (q V ~q)
12. (p & ~p) V (q & ~q)
13. ~[(p -&q) & ~(p V q)]
14. (p V q) V ~(p V q)
15. ~(p & q) V [(p V r) & (q V r)]
16. ~[~(p & q) V r] V [~p V (~q V r)]
17. (~p V ~p) & (p V p)
18. [(p & q) V (r & s)] V (~p V ~q)

E. Construct a truth table for each of the following statement forms, and determine whether the form is tautologous, self-contradictory, or contingent. (Wilson, p.83).

1. p ⊃ p
2. (p V q) ⊃ p
3. (p & q) ⊃ p
4. (p V q) & (~p & ~q)
5. (p ⊃ q) V (p ⊃ ~q)
6. p V (q ⊃ r)
7. [p V (q & r)] & ~[(p V q) & (p V r)]
8. [(p ⊃ q) & (r ⊃ s)] ⊃ [(~q V ~s) ⊃ (~p V ~r)]

F. Use truth tables to determine whether a substitution instance of each of the following statement forms would be a tautology, a contradiction, or a contingent statement. (Churchill, p. 249.)

1. p ⊃ (q ⊃ p)
2. (p V q) & (-p V -q)
3. ~p & (~q V p)
4. ~p V ~(q & ~r)
5. ~p & (~q & r)

4

6. ~[p ⊃ (p V q)]
7. (p & q) V (~p & ~q)
8. (p V q) & (~p V ~q)
9. (p & q) ⊃ (p V q)
10. (~p ⊃ p) & (p ⊃ ~p)
11. (p V q) ⊃ (p & q)
12. [(p V q) & (p & q)] ⊃ p
13. (p ⊃ ~p) ≡ ~p
14. [p & (p V q)] ≡ [p V (p & q)]
15. [p & (q V ~q)] ≡ p

H. Determine which of the following are tautologies, contradictions, contingencies (Manicus and Kruger, p.99.):

1. p ⊃ ~p
2. p V ~q
3. ~(p ⊃ p)
4. p ⊃ (p Vq)
5. p ≡ ~p
6. pq V (~p ⊃ ~ q)
7. pq ⊃ (p V q)
8. (p ⊃ q) (q ⊃ r) ⊃ (p ⊃ r)
9. (p V q)(pq) ⊃ p
10. (p V q) ⊃ ~q

I. Translate the following statements into the logical form of your choice and determine if each is a tautology, a contradiction , or a contingency. (Klein)

1. It is not the case that the food and the drinks will be set up by noon and it is not the case that if the food is set up, then the drinks will not be.

2. Joe and Ruth will get married to each other or they will not; if they do not marry each other, then Tim will probably go back out to sea.

3. The parents of the groom will show up to the wedding only if the sister of the bride is not present; alas, she will be present.

4. Either the flowers will arrive on time or they will not.

5. If Joe does not come back from sea, then either the wedding is off or it will have to be held at the courthouse.

J. For each sentence form, determine whether its tautologous, contradictory, or contingent. (McKay, p.59.)

1. p V q
2. (p & q) V ~p
3. ~(p & q) V p
4. (p V q) & ~(p & q)
5. (p V q) & (~p & ~q)
6. (p V p) & ~ p
7. (p & q) V (p V r)
8. ~(p & q) V [(r V p) & (r V q)]
9. (p & q) & ~(p V q)
10. p V (q V ~p)
11. (p V ~p) V q
12. (p V ~p) & q
13. (p V ~p) & (q V ~q)
14. (p & ~p) V (q & ~q)
15. (p V q) V ~(p V q)

K. Determine if each of the following are true or false. Explain. (Gustason, p.43.)

1. "If a conjunction is a tautology, then each of its conjuncts must also be a tautology."
2. "If the negation of a conjunction is a tautology and the negation of one of its conjuncts is a contradiction, then the other conjunct must be a contradiction."

Chapter Two

Logical Equivalencies[*]

A. Using truth-tables, show that the following pairs of sentence forms are equivalent (the same table may be used for more than one exercise.) (Gustason, p.43.)

1. p & q;   q & p
2. p V q;   q V p
3. p & (q & r);   (p & q) & r
4. p V (q V r);   (p V q) V r
5. p & (q V r);   (p & q) V (p & r)
6. p V (q & r);   (p V q) & (p V r)
7. p;   ~~p
8. ~p V ~q;   ~(p & q)

B. Indicate whether the sentence forms are *logically equivalent*. (McKay, p.75.)

1. p & q   2. ~p V q
   q & p   p V ~q

3. ~(p V q)   4. ~(p & q)
   ~p & ~q   ~p & ~q

5. ~(p V q)   6. p & (q & r)
   ~p & q   (r & p) & q

7. p & ~q   8. ~[p V (q V r)]
   ~(q V ~p)   ~p & (~q & ~r)

9. p V (q & r)   10. ~(p & q) & r
   (p V q) & r   ~p & (q & r)

11. ~[p V (q & r)]   12. ~[p & (q & r)]
    (~p & ~q) V (~p & ~r)   ~p V (~q & ~r)

---

[*] See the **Appendix** for a helpful template for use in doing the below exercises.

7

C. For each pair of sentence forms, determine whether they are equivalent. (McKay, p.56.)

1. p V q
   q V p

2. ~p V q
   p V ~q

3. ~(p & q)
   ~p V ~q

4. ~(p & q)
   ~p & ~q

5. p V (q V r)
   (p V q) V r

6. ~p V ~q
   ~(p V q)

7. ~p & q
   ~(p & q)

8. p V (q & r)
   (p V q) & r

8. ~(p & q) & r
   ~p & (q & r)

10. ~~(p V q)
    ~~p & ~~q

D. Show by truth tables that the following pairs are equivalent and identify in each the equivalent subparts that are substituted for each other. (Neidorff, p.151.)

1. P ⊃ (R v S) and P ⊃ [(R v S) v (T & ~T)]
2. P ⊃ (R & T and P ⊃ {[R v (R & S)] & T}
3. ~[P & (R v ~R)] and ~[P & ~~(S & ~S]
4. ~~[~(P v Q) & R] and ~[Q v (~R v P)]

E. We claim that the equivalence of P & Q and Q & P can be regarded as a *form* that can be invoked to justify the interchange of conjuncts in any context, even if the conjuncts are themselves molecules, [i.e., collections of individual statements.] Justify that claim.

F. Use truth tables to determine whether the compound statements in each of the following pairs are or are not truth-functionally equivalent (Churchill, p.248.)

    1.   a. If the board of trustees has the long-term interests of the college in mind, it will approve the increase in scholarship aid.
         b. Either the board of trustees does not have the long-term interests of the college in mind, or it will approve the increase in scholarship aid.

    2.   a. If the professors are to be prepared for their nine o'clock classes, they are now working in their offices.
         b. If the professors aren't now working in their offices, they are not going to be prepared for their nine o'clock classes.

G. Write the compound statements below in symbolic notation, using the letters indicated. Then write a logically equivalent statement for each such statement. (Halverson, p.180.)

Example:
    If it rains today, I cannot mow the lawn. (R, M)
    Symbolic statement: R ⊃ ~M
    Logically equivalent statement: ~R v ~M

    1. I am old and you are young. (O, Y)
    2. That I am old and you are young is not the case. (O, Y)
    3. Either I am not seeing clearly, or there is a kangaroo in my driveway. (S, K)
    4. I am not seeing clearly and that is not a kangaroo in my driveway. (S, K)
    5. I will try to parachute jumping only on the condition that you will too. (I, Y)
    6. It is not the case that the senator accepted the bribe, nor was there one offered. (A, O)
    7. Either the senator did not accept the bribe or else he did not know what he was doing. (A, K)
    8. I will go if you will drive. (G, D)
    9. We will go to Florida if and only if the check arrives. (F, C)
    10. That you ought to do it implies that you can do it. (O, C)

Chapter Three

Testing for Validity/Invalidity (Long Truth-Table*)

A. Explain how truth tables can be used to test the validity of sentential arguments. (Halverson, p.187.)

B. Determine by means of truth tables which of the following arguments and argument forms are valid and which are invalid. (Halverson, p.187.)

    1. A ⊃ B (B v C)
    2. ~B / ∴ C v ~A

    1. M ≡ (N • R)
    2. ~R ⊃ S / ∴ M v ~S

    1. A v B
    2. B v C / ∴ ~A ⊃ (A • C)

    1. S v L
    2. L v R / ∴ ~S v R

    1. (L ⊃ C) • (S ⊃ A)
    2. L • S / ∴ C v A

    1. p ⊃ ~q
    2. r ⊃ q / ∴ p V r

    1. p V (q • r)
    2. ~r / ∴ q

---

* See the **Appendix** for a helpful template for use in doing the below exercises.

1. p ⊃ (q • r)
2. ~p / ∴ ~(q • r)

1. p ⊃ q
2. ~q / ∴ ~p

1. p ⊃ q
2. q ⊃ r / ∴ p ⊃ r

C. For each of the argument forms shown below, indicate whether it is valid or invalid. ((McKay, pp.96-97.)

1. p ⊃ q
   q
  ∴ p

2. p ⊃ (q V r)
   q
  ∴ p

3. ~p
  ∴ ~(p • q)

4. p ⊃ (q ⊃ r)
  ∴ (p ⊃ q) ⊃ r

5. p V q
  r V s
  ∴ q ⊃ q

6. p V q
  ~q V r
  ~p V ~r
  ∴ q

7. p ⊃ q
  r ⊃ s
  p V r
  ∴ q V s

8. p ⊃ q
  s ⊃ r
  q V r
  ∴ p V s

9. p V q
  ~r V s
  r V ~s
  ∴ p V r

10. p • (q V r)
  ∴ (p • q) V r

11. p ⊃ q
  ~r ⊃ ~q
  ∴ p ⊃ ~r

12. p ⊃ (q • r)
  ∴ (p ⊃ q) • r

11

13. p ⊃ (q V ~p)
    q
    ∴ ~p

14. p V (q ≡ ~r)
    ~(q ⊃ p) • (r ⊃ p)
    ∴ r V p

15. p ≡ q
    ~ (q ≡ r)
    ∴ ~r ⊃ p

D. Which are valid? (McKay, p.61.)

1. p • q
    q V r
    ∴ ~(q • ~q)

2. p V q
    ~q V r
    ~ (p V r)
    ∴ p • ~r

2. p V ~q
    q V p
    ∴ q • p

4. p V ~p
    ~ (q • ~q)
    ∴ (p V q) • (~p • ~q)

5. p V q
    r V ~q
    p V r
    ∴ ~p V ~r

E. Construct a truth table for each of the following argument forms, and determine whether the argument form is valid. (Wilson, p.93.)

1. p V q
    p
    ∴ ~q

2. p V q
    ~p
    ∴ q

12

3. p ⊃ q
   ~p
   ∴ q

4. p q
   q V ~p
   ∴ p

5. ~(p & q)
   p
   ∴ ~q

6. p ⊃ q
   ~q V r
   ~r p
   ∴ ~p

7. ~p
   ~q V ~p
   ∴ r V ~p

8. p ⊃ (q V r)
   ~q & ~r
   ∴ ~p

9. p ⊃ q
   r ⊃ q
   q
   ∴ p V r

10. (p ⊃ q) & (r ⊃ s)
    p V r
    ∴ q V s

F. Use truth tables to prove that each of the following is a *valid* argument form. (Churchill, p.255.)

1. p ⊃ q
   p
   ∴ q

2. p ⊃ q
   ~q
   ∴ ~p

13

3. ~ (p & q)   4. p ⊃ q
   p   q ⊃ r
  ∴ ~q   ∴ p ⊃ r

5. p & q   6. p
  ∴ p   q
                 ∴ p & q

7. p   8. p ≡ q
  ∴ p V q   p
                 ∴ q

9. p ⊃ q   10. p ⊃ q
   r ⊃ s   r ⊃ s
   p V r   ~q V ~s
  ∴ q V s   ∴ ~p V ~r

G. Use truth tables to prove that each of the following is an *invalid* argument form. (Churchill, p.255.)

1. p ⊃ q   2. p ⊃ q
   q   ~p
  ∴ p   ∴ ~q

3. p V q   4. ~ (p & q)
   p   ~q
  ∴ ~q   ∴ p

5. ~ (p & q)   6. ~p V ~q
  ∴ ~p & ~q   ∴ ~ (p V q)

7. p ⊃ q   8. p ⊃ q
   q ⊃ r   q ⊃ r
  ∴ r ⊃ p   ∴ q ⊃ p

14

9. $p \equiv q$
   $\sim p$
   $\therefore q$

10. $p \supset q$
    $r \supset s$
    $q \lor s$
    $\therefore p \lor r$

H. In each case, use a truth table to show whether a sentence having the first form would truth-functionally imply a sentence having the second form.

1. $p \& q; q$

2. $q; q \lor p$

3. $p \& r; p \lor r$

4. $p; q \lor p$

5. $p; p \supset p$

6. $p \supset p; p$

7. $q; q \equiv q$

8. $q \equiv q; q$

9. $p \lor q; p \supset q$

10. $p \& q; p \supset q$

11. $\sim p; p \supset q$

12. $\sim p; p \equiv p$

13. $\sim(p \lor q); \sim q$

14. $\sim (p \& q); \sim q$

15. $\sim(p \supset q); p$

16. $\sim (p \supset q); \sim q$

17. $p \& q; p \equiv q$

18. $p \lor q; p \equiv q$

19.   p V q; p & q

20.   p ≡ q; p ⊃ q

I. Concept Reviews. (Wilson, p.95.)

   1. Relate the idea of "possibility", as expressed in the definition of truth tables, to whether an argument form is valid. How do the truth tables use possibilities in the definition of "valid"?

   2. We know that valid arguments cannot possibly have all true premises and a false conclusion. What combinations of truth and falsity are possible between the premises and the conclusions of *invalid* arguments?

Chapter Four

Testing for Validity/Invalidity (Short Truth-Table)

A. Symbolize each argument. Determine whether it is valid. (McKay, pp.100-101.)

1. Either they won't lower interest rates of they won't raise taxes. This is because if they lower interest rates, then there will be no federal revenue problem, and they will raise taxes only if there is a federal revenue problem. (L = Lower interest, R = Raise taxes, F =There will be a federal revenue problem)

2. If they lower interest rates and raise taxes, then there will be no federal revenue problem. But they won't lower taxes, so there will be a federal revenue problem. (L = Lower interest, R = Raise taxes, F = There will be a federal revenue problem)

3. They will raise taxes only if there is a federal revenue problem. If there is inflation, then there will be a federal revenue problem. So they will raise taxes. (R = Raise taxes, F = Federal revenue problem, I = Inflation)

4. If they lower the taxes, then if they increase the money supply, then there will be inflation. If there is inflation, the elderly will have a rough time. Thus if they increase the money supply, the elderly will have a rough time, since they will be lowering taxes. (L = Lower taxes, M = Increase money, I = Inflation, E = Elderly have a rough time)

5. The elderly will all have a rough time unless there are lower taxes and no inflation. There will be lower taxes. Thus the elderly will not all have a rough time. (E = The elderly all have a rough time, L = There are lower taxes, I = There is inflation)

6. The economy is going to be in big trouble, because it cannot tolerate a drastic drop in the stock market, but there will be one. (T = Economy in big trouble, D = There is a drastic drop in the stock market)

7. The president will be reelected only if the economy improves. The economy will improve only if foreign nations cooperate. Thus the president will not be reelected, because foreign nations will not cooperate. (R = The president is reelected, E = The economy improves, F = Foreign nations cooperate)

8. If inflation increases, the elderly will be in financial difficulty. If taxes increase, young adults will be in financial difficulty. If young adults and the elderly are both in financial difficulty, the president will not be reelected. Thus if the president is to be reelected, inflation must not increase or taxes must not increase. (I= Inflation increases, E =Elderly in difficulty, T= Taxes increase, Y= Young adults in difficulty, R= The president is reelected)

B. Test the validity of the following arguments and argument forms by means of abbreviated truth tables (Halverson, p.191.)

1. 1. (A ⊃ B) & (C ⊃ D)
   2. A & ~D / ∴ B & C

2. 1. A v (B v C)
   2. ~C ⊃ D / ∴ A v D

3. 1. (G & K) ⊃ P
   2. M ⊃ (S & ~P) / ∴ M ⊃ ~(G & K)

4. 1. (F ⊃ R) & (F v B)
   2. ~B / ∴ R

5. 1. (L ≡ S) ⊃ (W & B)
   2. ~ (L ≡ S) / ∴ ~(W & B)

6. 1. p ⊃ (q ⊃ r)
   2. [r V ~(s ≡ t)] & ~r / ∴ p ⊃ (s ≡ t)

7. 1. (p V q) ⊃ r
   2. ~r / ∴ ~p & ~q

8. 1. p ⊃ q
   2. q ⊃ r / ∴ r V ~p

9. 1. p ⊃ (q ≡ r)
   2. r ⊃ (s V t) / ∴ p ⊃ s

10. 1. (p V q) ⊃ (r & s)
    2. p & ~q / ∴ r ≡ s

C. Using the method of assigning truth-values, determine whether the following arguments are valid (Gustason, pp.66-67):

1. E ⊃ (J & K)
   F ⊃ (E v A)
   ~K / ∴ F ⊃ J

2. A ⊃ (B & C)
   B ⊃ (~A & C) / ∴ ~A

18

3. A ⊃ E
   B ⊃ F
   ~E v ~F / ∴ ~A v ~B

4. M v N
   L v K
   (M v L) ⊃ (N & K) / ∴ N & K

5. (A & C) ⊃ F
   (B & F) ⊃ [~E ⊃ (D v ~A)] / ∴ (A & B) ⊃ [C ⊃ (D v E)]

6. A ⊃ (B ⊃ C)
   D ⊃ (B & A)
   C ⊃ D / ∴ C ≡ A

7. If Irv does not prove the continuum hypothesis, then although Karl will not gloat, Henry will. However, neither Karl nor Henry will gloat. Consequently, if Irv proves the continuum hypothesis only if Karl gloats, then Irv in fact proves the continuum hypothesis.

8. If the President vetoes the trade bill, Congress will either back him up or else succumb to public pressure. Japan will not raise its tariffs unless the protectionists have their way. If the protectionists have their way and Congress succumbs to public pressure, the world markets will be in disarray. The President did in fact veto the trade bill, so if Japan raises its tariffs, then Congress will not back up the President and the world markets will be in disarray.

9. Milo buys eggs in Sicily at I cent per egg and sells them to the distributors in Malta at 41 cents per egg, and if he does both he clears 31 cents per egg. If Milo buys eggs in Sicily at I cent per egg and buys them back from the distributors in Malta for 7 cents, then he pays a total of 8 cents per egg. If Milo clears 34 cents per egg and sells them to the commissary for 5 cents, then he takes in N cents per egg. If Milo pays a total of 8 cents per egg and takes in a total of 81cents per egg, then he makes a profit. Consequently, if Milo buys back eggs from the distributors in Malta at 7 cents per egg and sells them to the commissary for 5 cents, then he makes a profit.

D. Use the short truth-table method to determine if the following are valid or invalid (Neidorff, pp.140141)

1. If mercy or charity is a virtue, Eloise is virtuous. Mercy is a virtue. Hence, Eloise is virtuous.

2. Mercy is not a virtue unless charity is not a virtue. It is not the case that mercy is not a virtue. Therefore, charity is not a virtue.

3. Mercy is a virtue unless vindictiveness is. Mercy is not a virtue and cruelty is a vice. Were vindictiveness a virtue, so would selfishness be. Therefore, selfishness is a virtue.

4. Harry will go or Manuel will not, but Gene will definitely go. If Harry goes his wife will accompany him. But his wife will not go. If Joseph goes so will Manuel. Hence, Joseph will not go.

5. If the rose wins Mrs. Miniver will be pleased. If the aster wins she will be put out. If the judge is not competent either the rose or aster will win. If the judge is competent the prize will not even be awarded. It is not the case that the prize will not be awarded. Hence, Mrs. Miniver will be pleased or put out.

6. If Mrs. Miniver is pleased provided the rose wins, and she is in a normally good humor, then the gardener will get a week off. If her husband is not here or her brother is, she will be in a normally good humor. If her husband is here, the judges will be intimidated. The judges will not be intimidated, and Mrs. Miniver will be pleased. The judges will be intimidated, unless Mrs. Miniver is pleased provided the rose wins. Thus, the gardener will get a week off.

7. If the car is sound, then if the driver lasts it out they will come in first. If the fees are paid, then if the shares are fair they will receive a tidy sum. The car is sound. And the fees are paid. Provided the car is sound and the fees are paid, nothing can go wrong. If nothing goes wrong, then either the driver will last it out or the shares will be fair, perhaps both. Hence, they will come in first or receive a tidy sum, perhaps both.

8. If all three animals survive, the serum is effective. If there is movement in the first cage, the first animal has survived. If there is a sign of escape in the second cage, the second animal has survived. And if there are noises in the third cage, the third animal has survived. There is movement in the first cage, a sign of escape in the second, noise in the third, and a healthy animal in the fourth. Hence, the serum is effective.

9. A sufficient condition for the serum's not being effective is that if the animal was not treated, he survived. If the serum is effective, all animals are dead or dying. But not all treated animals are dead or dying. If it is not the case that this animal survived if he was not treated, then further inquiry is useless. Hence, further inquiry is useless.

10. There will be a sea fight tomorrow. There will not be a sea fight tomorrow. Therefore, the serum is effective.

E. For each of these argument forms, determine whether it is *valid* or *invalid*. (McKay, p.50)

1. p V q
   ~q / ∴ p

2. p / ∴ p V q

3. p V q
   p / ∴ ~q

20

4. p & q
   ~p V r / ∴ p & r

5. p V q
   ~q V r / ∴ p V r

6. p V q
   ~p V r / ∴ p & r

7. ~(p & q)
   p V r / ∴ ~q V r

8. ~(p & r)
   p / ∴ ~r

F. Translate and determine if the following arguments are valid or invalid (Neidorff, pp.128-129):

1. The train will be on time. If it is, Mr. Smith will catch the plane to Washington. The passage of the Smith Bill will guarantee that the dam will be built. His bill will be passed if he catches the plane to Washington. So the dam will be built after all.

2. If only the relay works, then the temperature will stay up if the generator does not fail. If the generator does not fad, the relay will work. The maintenance staff is not lazy. And the generator win fail only if the maintenance staff is lazy. Hence, the temperature will stay up.

3. Good rain this month is a necessary condition for a decent corn harvest. If there is a decent corn harvest and a reasonable market, we will make enough for a new tractor or a down payment on the house we want. If there is not a decent corn harvest, we will not make enough for a new tractor or a down payment on the new house. There will not be any rain this month. So, there will not be both a decent corn harvest and a reasonable market.

4. Frisbee will join a fraternity if they are democratic. They are democratic. Hence, Frisbee will join.

5. Frisbee will join a fraternity only if they are democratic. They are democratic. Hence, Frisbee will join.

6. Frisbee will join a fraternity if and only if they are democratic. They are democratic. Hence, Frisbee will join.

7. Only if fraternities are democratic will Frisbee join. They are democratic. Hence, Frisbee will join.

8. If and only if fraternities are democratic Frisbee will join. As they are democratic, it follows that he will join.

21

9. The enemy will come through the pass if and only if we abandon the forward line. We will abandon the forward line if and only if our supplies fail. Hence, the enemy will come through the pass if and only if our supplies fail.

10. The enemy will come through the pass only if we abandon the forward line. We will abandon the forward line if our supplies fail. Hence, the enemy will come through the pass only if our supplies fail.

11. The enemy will come through the pass only if we abandon the forward line. We will abandon the forward line only if our supplies fail. Hence, the enemy will come through the pass only if our supplies fail.

12. Chicago is west of Detroit if and only if Evanston is west of Denver. It is not the case that: Either Evanston is west of Denver or east of Joliet (but not both). Therefore, Chicago is west of Detroit only if Evanston is east of Joliet.

13. The solution to the equation is an answer to the problem only if the equation has been properly set up. But the equation has indeed been properly set up. Therefore, the solution to the equation is an answer to the problem.

G. For each of the following arguments, use the short-cut method to show that it is invalid (Barker, pp. 102)

    1. $C \supset D, D, \therefore C$
    2. $F \lor G, F, \therefore \sim G$
    3. $\sim(A \& B), \sim A, \therefore \sim B$
    4. $A \supset \sim B, \sim A \& B, \sim A, \therefore B$
    5. $D \supset E, E \supset G, F \supset G, \therefore D \& F$
    6. $C \supset D, \sim C \supset \sim A, \sim D \supset \sim B, \therefore \sim B \supset \sim A$
    7. $A \supset B, C \supset D, B \lor D, \therefore A \lor C$
    8. $F \supset G, H \supset K, \sim F \lor \sim H, \therefore \sim G \lor \sim K$
    9. $A \supset (C \& D), (B \lor C) \supset D, \therefore D \& A$
    10. $K \supset (L \supset M), F \supset (G \lor H), G \supset (K \lor L), \sim(F \& M) \therefore F \& H$

H. For each argument show either that the argument is valid or that it is invalid (Barker, pp.102-103)

1. If the seal has not been broken and the routine servicing has been performed, the guarantee is in effect. The owner is responsible for the damage only if the routine servicing has not been performed or the seal has been broken. Hence, the guarantee is in effect unless the owner is responsible for the damage.

22

2. Either Thales said nothing moves and Parmenides didn't say it, or else Parmenides said it and Heraclitus denied it. If Thales said it, his thought didn't conform to the Milesian pattern. Thales' thought did conform to the Milesian pattern. Therefore, Heraclitus denied that nothing moves.

3. If either revenues increase or debt and costs decrease, the firm's profitability will improve. Costs won't decrease unless debt decreases. It's not the case both that revenues will increase and that profitability will improve. Therefore, either debts won't decrease or profitability will improve.

4. If Locke had denied the existence of spiritual substance, he would have been a materialist; if he had denied the existence of physical substance, he would have been an idealist. If he had been either an idealist or a materialist, he would not have been a dualist. But Locke was a dualist. Therefore, he did not deny the existence of either spiritual or physical substance.

5. If Moses and Abraham were patriarchs, then Samuel and Jeremiah were prophets. If Abraham was a patriarch, Samuel was a prophet. Therefore, either Moses was not a patriarch or Jeremiah was not a prophet.

I. Analyze the structure of each of the following truth-functional arguments. Watch for unstated premises. (Barker, p.102)

1. "1 hope, Marianne," continued Elinor, "you do not consider Edward as deficient in general taste. Indeed, I think I may say that you cannot, for your behavior to him is perfectly cordial, and if that were your opinion, I am sure you could never be civil to him." JANE AUSTEN, *Sense and Sensibility.*

2. Murder and treachery cannot be good without regret being bad: regret cannot be good without treachery and murder being bad, Both, however, are supposed to have been foredoomed; so something must be fatally unreasonable, absurd, and wrong in the world. It must be a place of which either sin or error forms a necessary part. From this dilemma there seems at first sight no escape. WILLIAM JAMES, "The Dilemma of Determinism"

J. Symbolize each of the following arguments using the suggested letters. Construct truth tables to determine whether each argument has a valid or invalid argument form. (Churchill, pp.255-256)

1. Either the birthrate in Mexico will decline, or Mexico will face an economic Crisis. So it is not the case that either the birthrate in Mexico won't decline or that Mexico won't face an economic crisis. (B, E)

2. It is not true that both the price of gold is fixed and that people speculate on the price. People do speculate on the price of gold. Consequently, it is not fixed. (G, S)
Either Shirley will get her degree in May, or she will drop out of school and take a job with her mother. If I know her, she will not drop out of school. Consequently, she will get her degree. (D, S, J)

3. If grade inflation is to cease, grade anxiety among students must decrease. If grade inflation ceases, then standardized test scores will become less important in law-school admissions. Thus if grade anxiety among students decreases, standardized test scores will become less important in law-school admissions. (G, A, S)

4. If the testimony of the witness was correct, the defendant was guilty. The defendant was indeed guilty. So the testimony of the witness must have been correct. (T, D)

5. If there is an indictment, then if he is brought to trial he will be convicted. But he won't be brought to trial. So, either there will be an indictment or he will be convicted. (I, B, C)

6. Either the maid is guilty or the governess is lying. If the maid is guilty, Lady Poultney was murdered for her diamond tiara. The governess is not lying. Therefore, Lady Poultney was murdered for her diamond tiara. (M, G, P)

7. If the economic theory of Adam Smith is unsound, then so is that of Thomas Malthus. If the economic theory of David Ricardo is unsound, then so is that of Smith. So if the economic theory of Malthus is sound that of Ricardo is also sound. (S, M, R)

8. If Sam got an A in Spanish, he must have worked hard and paid attention in class. But it is false that he worked hard and paid attention in class. So he didn't get an A in Spanish. (S, W, P)

9. If the high-pressure system has moved in, the weather back home is clear and the temperatures are warm. But because the system has not moved in, the weather must be either cloudy or cool. (H, C, T)

10. Either the president is happy and the college has been accredited, or the president is happy and the endowment was increased. The president is happy. The endowment was not increased. Therefore, the college was accredited. (P, C, E)

11. Stephanie is a lawyer only if she hasn't been disbarred. It's not the case that she hasn't been disbarred. So Stephanie isn't a lawyer. (L, D)

12. If he passed the bar exam, he has graduated from law school. He is a lawyer if and only if he passed the bar exam and graduated from law school. So either he isn't a lawyer, or he passed the bar exam. (P, G, L)

13. If the drought continues, then the crops will fail. If the crops fail, the farmers will be ruined. But if the state is declared a disaster area, the farmers will not be ruined, The drought will continue and the state will be declared a disaster area. Therefore, the farmers will not be ruined. (D, C, F, S)

14. If East Germany develops closer ties with West Germany, then the Polish people will demand greater liberalization within their own country. If the Polish people demand greater liberalization, then the Soviet Union will risk social unrest by increasing its military presence in Poland. But the Soviet Union won't risk social unrest by increasing its military presence in Poland. Therefore, East Germany won't develop closer ties with West Germany. (E, P, S)

K. Check the following for validity (Manicas and Kruger, p.94):

1. p V q
   p / ∴ q

2. p V ~q
   q / ∴ p

3. p ⊃ q
   p / ∴ q

4. pq ≡ r
   p V ~r / ∴ q

5. (p V q)~(pq)
   p / ∴ q

L. Check the following for validity (Manicas and Kruger, pp.103-104)

1. pq V r
   ~(pq)(r ≡ t) / ∴ u

2. p ≡ q
   q ≡ r
   p V s / ∴ p ≡ s

3. (p ~q)r
   ~p V ~r
   q ⊃ s / ∴ q V s

4. pqr V pq~r
   p ⊃ q
   q ⊃ s / ∴ ps

5. p V q V r
   ~(pr)
   r ⊃ (s V t) / ∴ ~s ⊃ t

6. p ⊃ q
   r ⊃ p
   s V r / ∴ q~s

M. Check the following arguments for validity by the indirect truth-table technique. (Neidorff, pp.97-98)

1. If death is a pleasant dream we have nothing to fear. If death is a long sleep we have nothing to fear. Death is a pleasant dream or a long sleep Therefore, we have nothing to fear.

2. Either death is a pleasant dream and if it is we have nothing to fear, or death is a long sleep and if it is we have nothing to fear. Therefore, we have nothing to fear.

3. Either we have nothing to fear if death is a pleasant dream or we have nothing to fear if death is a long sleep. Therefore, we have nothing to fear.

4. If Descartes is right the mind does not occupy space. If the mind does not occupy space it is immaterial. If it is immaterial it is not subject to decay. If it is not subject to decay it is immortal. Descartes is right. Therefore, the mind is immortal.

5. If Aquinas was right, reason is dependable. If reason is dependable, then Aquinas' proofs for the existence of God are sound. If Aquinas' proofs for the existence of God are sound, then Kant is wrong. If Kant is wrong then so is Newton. Newton is right. Therefore, Aquinas was wrong.

6. If it is true that if prices generally rise then all salaries rise, then if steel prices go up so will steel wages. Prices will generally rise, and not all salaries will rise. If steel prices go up new car prices will decline. If steel wages do not go up appliance purchases will decline. And if appliance purchases and new car sales decline, we are in for a recession. Therefore, steel prices will go up, and we are in for a recession.

7. If the solution is dilute and the mice do not overeat, then if they got the supplement they will survive. Either the colorimeter is badly calibrated or the solution is dilute. Yet, if the colorimeter is badly calibrated then, still, the solution is dilute. If the mice overeat, then it is not the case that they will either be hungry or frustrated. It is certainly not true that either they will survive or they will not be hungry. Therefore, they did not get the supplement.

8. If the Patagonians have heavy artillery within range, then, in the first place, it is not the case that they will either miss the chance to use it or avoid the consequent test of strength, and in the second place, if they do not miss the chance to use it they will come over Sinbad's Ridge and deploy in the heights beyond. Hence, if they have heavy artillery within range, then they will not avoid the consequent test of strength and they will deploy in the heights beyond Sinbad's Ridge.

26

9. If it is not true that if most prices rise steel prices rise, then if steel prices rise wages will be stable. Most prices will rise, and steel prices will not rise. If steel prices do not rise, appliance purchases will fall off. If appliance purchases fall off and wages remain stable, we are in for a recession. Therefore, we are in for a recession and most prices will rise.

10. It is false that Mary will go and John will not. If the car will be on time, then either John will go or Mary will. The driver will be sober.

11. If the pea is under the first shell, then if I have been watching I have been fooled. If I have been fooled, my eyes have lost their sharpness. If my eyes have lost their sharpness, I have not been taking proper care of them. If I have been taking proper care of them, then I have been using the right glasses. If my oculist made a mistake, then I have not been using the right glasses. The pea is under the first shell. Therefore, if I have been watching, then my oculist made a mistake.

N. Answer the following questions—model or use examples if necessary (Neidorff, p.98)

1. Is the indirect truth table technique a decision procedure?
2. How can you adapt the indirect truth-table technique to test sets of propositions for consistency? Test the premises in exercises above.

3. Suppose the indirect truth-table technique is used to test an argument containing **n** premises for validity. There is a sense in which, at the same time, a set in **n** + 1 propositions is being tested for consistency. Explain.

4. Which of the following are correct?
   a. In a valid argument, the truth of the premises is a necessary condition for the truth of the conclusion.
   b. In a valid argument, the truth of the conclusion is a necessary condition for the truth of the premises.
   c. In a valid argument, the truth of the premises is a sufficient condition for the truth of the conclusion.
   d. In a valid argument, the truth of the conclusion is a sufficient condition for the truth of the premises.

Chapter Five

Rules of Inference Part I, The "Eight Rules" (Partially Completed)

A. Each of the following is a completed formal proof for the indicated argument. Indicate the inferential form, and the lines used, for each derived line. In each case, try to view the inferential form in terms of its formal proof effects. Look at this set of exercises as a means to help you with the next set. Your goal should be to construct formal proofs yourself! (Wilson, pp.123-124.)

1. 1. (B v V) ⊃ C
   2. B / ∴ C
   3. B v V
   4. C

2. 1. A
   2. B
   3. (A & B) ⊃ C / ∴ C
   4. A & B
   5. C

3. 1. ~V & D / ∴ ~V v D
   2. ~V
   3. ~V v D

4. 1. (B v V) ⊃ (D -& C)
   2. B / ∴ C
   3. B v V
   4. D & C

5. 1. A ⊃ B
   2. (B v C) ⊃ D
   3. A / ∴ D
   4. B
   5. B v C
   6. D

6. 1. B & V
   2. [(V v C) & D] ⊃ (T ⊃ W)
   3. T & D / ∴ W
   4. V
   5. V v C
   6. D
   7. (V v C) & D
   8. T ⊃ W
   9. T
   10. W

7. 1. B ⊃ V
   2. B ⊃ (D & C)
   3. [V & (D & C)] ⊃ (R & T)
   4. B / ∴ T
   5. V
   6. D & C
   7. V & (D & C)
   8. R & T
   9. T

B. Stated below are several valid arguments, each followed by a formal proofs, of validity. Justify each statement in the proof. (Halverson, p.202.)

1. 1. K ⊃ L
   2. M ⊃ N
   3. (L v N) ⊃ Z
   4. K v M / ∴ Z
   5. (K ⊃ L) & (M ⊃N)
   6. L v N
   7. Z

2. 1. W ⊃ B
   2. B ⊃ L
   3. (W & L) ⊃ C
   4. W / ∴ C
   5. W ⊃ L
   6. L
   7. W & L
   8. C

3. 1. A & (B v C)
    2. A ⊃ ~B / ∴ C
    3. A
    4. ~B
    5. B v C
    6. C

4. 1. (L ⊃ T) & (~L ⊃ Z)
    2. ~T / ∴ Z
    3. L ⊃ T
    4. ~L
    5. ~L ⊃ Z
    6. Z

5. 1. A v (S ≡ L)
    2. (S ≡ L) ⊃ R
    3. ~R / ∴ A
    4. ~(S ≡ L)
    5. A

6. 1. B ⊃ V
    2. R ⊃ X
    3. (V v X) ⊃ Q
    4. B / ∴ Q
    5. (B ⊃ V) & (R ⊃ X)
    6. B v R
    7. V v X
    8. Q

7. 1. (A ≡ B) ⊃ (C & D)
    2. (C & D) ⊃ (R v Q)
    3. (A ≡ B)
    4. (R ⊃ L) & (Q ⊃ T)
    5. (L v T) ⊃ X / ∴ X
    6. (A ≡ B) ⊃ (R v Q)
    7. A ≡ B
    8. R v Q
    9. (R ⊃ L) & (Q ⊃ T)
    10. L v T
    11. X

8. 1. (B ⊃ R) & (G ⊃ P)
    2. ~(B v ~G) ⊃ L
    3. ~R / ∴ L
    4. B ⊃ R
    5. ~B
    6. ~B v ~G

C. Complete each of the following deductions by applying the designated rules to the lines indicated. (Churchill, pp.273-275.)

(1)
    1. A & ~B   Premise
    2. A ⊃ (B V C) / ∴ C   Premise/Conclusion
    3.   (1), Simp.
    4.   (2), (3), M. P.
    5.   (1), Simp.
    6.   (4), (5), Disi. Arg.

(2)
    1. (A v B) ⊃ C   Premise
    2. D ⊃ (Av B)   Premise
    3. ~D ⊃ ~E   Premise
    4. ~C / ∴ ~E   Premise/Conclusion
    5.   (1), (4), M.P.
    6.   (2), (5), M.T.
    7.   (3), (6), M.P.

(3)
    1. ~F ⊃ ~G   Premise
    2. F ⊃ H   Premise
    3. J ⊃ K   Premise
    4. ~H & ~K / ∴ ~G & ~J   Premise/Conclusion
    5.   (4), Simp.
    6.   (3), (5), M.T.
    7.   (4), Simp.
    8.   (2), (7), M.T.
    9.   (1), (8), M.P.
    10.   (9), (6), Adj.

(4)
    1. F v G   Premise
    2. (F ⊃ ~H) & (K ⊃ ~G)   Premise
    3. K / ∴ ~H   Premise/Conclusion
    4.   (2), Simp.
    5.   (3), (4), M.P.
    6.   (1), (5), Disj. Arg.
    7.   (2), Simp.
    8.   (7), (6), M.P.

(5)
	1. (L v M) ⊃ N	Premise
	2. (N v 0) ⊃ (P v Q)	Premise
	3. L & ~P / ∴ Q	Premise/Conclusion
	4.	(3), Simp.
	5.	(4), Disj. Add.
	6.	(1), (5), M.P.
	7.	(6), Disj. Add.
	8.	(2), (7), M.P.
	9.	(3), Simp.
	10.	(8), (9), Disj. Arg.

(6)
	1. (L v M) ⊃ (N v 0)	Premise
	2. N ⊃ P	Premise
	3. L & ~P / ∴ 0 v R	Premise/Conclusion
	4.	(3), Simp.
	5.	(4), Disj. Add.
	6.	(1), (5), M.P.
	7.	(3), Simp.
	8.	(2), (7), M.T.
	9.	(6), (8), Disi. Arg.
	10.	(9), Disj. Add.

(7)
	1. (Q & R) ⊃ ~S	Premise
	2. P ⊃ (Q & R)	Premise
	3. (P ⊃ ~S) ≡ ~(~S) / ∴ ~P	Premise/Conclusion
	4.	(2), (1), Chain
	5.	(3), (4), Bicon. Arg.
	6.	(1), (5), M.T.
	7.	(2), (6), M.T.

(8)
	1. (P & Q) ⊃ ~R	Premise
	2. Q & (S v T)	Premise
	3. T ⊃ R	Premise
	4. S ⊃W	Pemise
	5. P ≡ Q / ∴ S	Premise/Conclusion
	6.	(2), Simp.
	7.	(4), (3), (6), C. D.
	8.	(2), Simp.
	9.	(5), (8), Bicon. Arg.
	10.	(9), (8), Adj.
	11.	(1), (10), M.P.
	12.	(3), (11), M. T.
	13.	(6), (12), Disj. Arg.

(9)

	1. W & X	Premise
	2. V ⊃ (S & T)	Premise
	3. ~[(W v Y) & (S & T)]	Premise
	4. ~V ⊃ Z / ∴ X & Z	Premise/Conclusion
	5.	(1), Simp.
	6.	(1), Simp.
	7.	(6), Disj. Add.
	8.	(3), (7), Conj. Arg.
	9.	(2), (8), M.T.
	10.	(4), (9), M.P.
	11.	(5), (10), Adj.

(10)

	1. ~S ⊃ (T ⊃ W)	Premise
	2. (T ⊃ W) ⊃ (W ⊃ X)	Premise
	3. (T ⊃ W) ⊃ [Y ⊃ (X ⊃ Z)]	Premise
	4. Y	Premise
	5. ~S / ∴ T ⊃ Z	Premise/Conclusion
	6.	(1), (5), M.P.
	7.	(2), (6), M.P.
	8.	(3), (6), M.P.
	9.	(8), (4), M.P.
	10.	(6), (7), Chain
	11.	(10), (9), Chain

33

Chapter Six

Rules of Inference Part II, The "Eight Rules"

A. Each of the following arguments makes an inference that is warranted by one of the elementary valid argument forms [i.e., inferences rules]. Identify the argument form that warrants each inference. (Halverson, p.197)

1. 1 B ⊃ Q
   2 R   /∴ R & (B ⊃ Q)

2. 1 (K & L) ≡ (M & R)
   2 K & L   /∴ M & R

3. 1 A ⊃ (B v R)
   2 (B v R) ⊃ (C ≡ K)   /∴ A ⊃ (C ≡ K)

4. B ≡ (Z v R)   /∴ [B ≡ (Z v R)] v (Z ⊃ K)

5. 1 A ≡ (X & Q)
   2 R ⊃ Z   /∴ [A ≡ (X & Q)] & (R ⊃ Z)

6. 1 (A ≡ X) ⊃ ~(L v Z)
   2 ~~(L v Z)   /∴ ~(A ≡ X)

7. (A ⊃ K) & (R v L)   /∴ A ⊃ K

8. 1 (A ≡ Z) ⊃ [R & (K v D)]
   2 A ≡ Z   /∴ R & (K v D)

9. 1 Z ⊃ [(A v B) & (C D)]
   2 [(A v B) & (C D)] ⊃ L   /∴ Z ⊃ L

10. 1 (K ⊃ Z) v ~(L & R)
    2 ~~(L & R)   /∴ K ⊃ Z

11. 1 (B & R) ⊃ (Q & S)
    2 ~(Q & S)   /∴ ~(B & R)

12. 1 K v (A ≡ B)
    2 ~K   /∴ A ≡ B

13. 1 (L v K) [S v ~(B & S)]
    2 L v K   /∴S v ~(B & S)

B. Using only two of the rules of inference, construct a formal proof for each of the following (Wilson, p. 125.)

1. T
   (T v W) ⊃ A
   ∴A

2. U
   P
   ∴(U v D) & P

3. H
   S
   ∴(H & S) v I

4. I & F
   I ⊃ H
   ∴H

5. D & P
   ∴D v T

6. (A & D) ⊃ F
   A & D
   N
   ∴F & N

7. R ⊃ V
   R
   ∴V v L

8. O
   S
   (O & S) ⊃ D
   ∴D

9. A & U
   P
   ∴A & P

10. C ⊃ (O & L)
    C
    ∴O

11. M & T
    ∴M v E

12. A & N
    M & S
    [(A & N) & (M & S)] ⊃ C
    ∴C

13. B ⊃ E
    [(B ⊃ E) v (P & H)] ⊃ M
    ∴M

14. J
    ~P
    ∴(~P v ~S) & J

15. F v T
     (F v T) ⊃ [(L ⊃ I) & (R v E)]
     ∴ R v E

C. For each of the following formal proofs of validity, provide the justification from each line which is not a premise. Identify the line or lines used and the appropriate rule of inference. (Manicus and Kruger, pp. 119-120.)

    1. 1. p ⊃ (q ⊃ r)
        2. s V p
        3. ~st / ∴ q ⊃ r
        4. ~s
        5. p
        6. p ⊃ (q ⊃ r)

    2. 1. p ⊃ q
        2. r ⊃ s
        3. (p V r) ~q / ∴ q V s
        4. (p ⊃ q)(r ⊃ s)
        5. p V r
        6. q V s

    3. 1. pq
        2. (p V r) (s V t) / ∴ p (s V t)
        3. p
        4. p V r
        5. s V t
        6. p (s V t)

    4. 1. (p V q) ⊃ r
        2. (r V q) ⊃ [p ⊃ (s ⊃t)]
        3. ps / ∴ s ⊃t
        4. p
        5. p V r
        6. r
        7. r V q
        8. p ⊃ (s ⊃ t)

    5. 1. p ⊃ ~q
        2. ~q ⊃ ~r
        3. ~~r   / ∴ ~p
        4. ~~q
        5. ~p

36

6. 1. p ⊃ ~q
   2. ~p ⊃ (r ≡ ~q)
   3. (~s V ~r) ⊃ ~~q
   4. ~s V ~r   /∴ r ≡ ~q
   5. ~~q
   6. ~p
   7. r ≡ ~q

D. Construct a formal proof of validity for each of the following arguments (Wilson, pp.126-127.)

1. (S & T) ⊃ C
   S
   T
   C

2. (S v T) ⊃ (C & D)
   S
   C

3. S & T
   (T v W) C
   C

4. A ⊃ B
   (B v C) ⊃ ~T
   A
   ~T

5. U
   U ⊃ (A & E)
   (A & R) ⊃ T
   R
   T

6. J & D
   (D v C) ⊃ T
   T v S

7. (E & U) & ~D
   (E & ~D) ⊃ R
   R

8. F ⊃ (A ⊃ ~E)
   F & A
   ~E

9. (A v F) ⊃ [(B v T) ⊃ R]
   A
   B
   R

10. I & W
    I ⊃ (T & V)
    (W & T) ⊃ R
    R

37

11.   T
     W
     (T & W) ⊃ R
     B
     V
     <u>(B & V) ⊃ D</u>
     D & R

12.   ~O ⊃ ~B
     ~I ⊃ ~C
     <u>~O & ~I</u>
     ~B & ~C

13.   A
     A ⊃ (V R)
     (R v T) ⊃ (C & D)
     <u>V</u>
     C

14.   ~I & (R ⊃ G)
     (R & G) ⊃ D
     <u>R</u>
     G & D

15.   (B ⊃ V) & (D ⊃ C)
     (B V) ⊃ ~(R v S)
     <u>[~(R v S) v (~R & ~S)] ⊃ U</u>
     U

16.   ~(A & V)
     ~(A & V) [T ⊃ (U & ~R)]
     U v (~V ⊃ W)] ⊃ (~W & ~R)
     <u>T</u>
     ~W

17.   ~(M ⊃ T)
     [(~M ⊃ T) & (S v F)] ⊃ (E ⊃ N)
     U ⊃ (S & E)
     <u>U</u>
     N

18.   ~(E & H) ⊃ (D & F)
     (A & ~O) ⊃ (W & B)
     [(D & F) v U] ⊃ A
     ~(E & H)
     <u>[(D & F) v U] ⊃ ~O</u>
     B

19.   (U & A) ⊃ (H & C)
     (Q v S) ⊃ U
     <u>(Q v T) & (A & Q)</u>
     H v C

20.   [(A & B) ⊃ (R & N)] & [(D v C) ⊃ T]
     <u>(A & B) & D</u>
     R & T

E. Translate the following into symbolic form and then construct a formal proof of validity. (Manicas and Kruger, pp. 120-121.)

1. If Sam gets an A in Spanish, he must have studied and hard and paid attention in class. But it is false that he studied hard and paid attention in class, so he I didn't get an A in Spanish. (p = Sam gets an A; q = Sam must have studied hard; r = Sam paid attention in class.)

2. If Sally won the prize, then Jane didn't. But if Jane didn't, then Harry lost his bet. Harry lost his bet only if Sam tricked him, and Sam didn't trick him unless Harry lost his head. But Harry didn't lose his head. Therefore, Sally didn't win the prize. (p = Sally won the prize; q = Jane won the prize; r = Harry lost his bet; s = Sam tricked Harry; t = Harry lost his head.)

3. If either Edith went to Detroit or took Sally with her on the trip, she took the train. If she took the train, she didn't fly. But if she didn't fly, she must have left Tuesday. Edith went to Detroit and had a nice time. So she must have left Tuesday. (p = Edith went to Detroit; q = Edith took Sally; r = Edith took the train; s = Edith flew; ~ t = Edith must have left Tuesday; u = Edith had a nice time.)

4. If universities charge no tuition everyone will enter. If universities charge tuition, there is not equal opportunity unless deserving students get scholarships But universities must either not charge tuition or charge tuition. Moreover, it is false that everyone will enter universities. Accordingly, if there is equality of opportunity, then deserving students get scholarships. (p= universities charge tuition; q =everyone will enter; r = there is equality of opportunity; s = deserving students get scholarships.)

5. If the world is chaos, then it cannot be reformed unless a sage appears. But no sage can appear if the world is chaos. The world surely is chaos; hence it cannot be reformed. (p = the world is chaos; q = the world can be reformed; r = a sage appears.)

F. Construct a proof for each of the following valid argument forms. (Manicaus and Kruger, p.120.)

1. 1. p V (q ⊃ r)
   2. ~pq
   3. q~s / ∴ r

2. 1. (p ⊃ q) ⊃ rs
   2. rs ⊃ (t ≡ u)
   3. ~(t ≡ u) / ∴ ~ (p ⊃ q)

3. 1. (p ⊃ qr)(r ⊃ st)
   2. p / ∴ qr V st

4. 1. p ⊃ qr
   2. s ⊃ t
   3. p V s
   4. ~(qr) / ∴ t

G. Translate the following into symbolic form and then construct a formal proof of validity for each of the following arguments. (Halverson, pp.184.)

1. If I stay on campus and study during spring vacation, I will not go home. If I do not go home, I will not be able to look for a summer job. If I am not able to look for a summer job, then either I will have no job or I will find a low-paying job later. If I have no job, I cannot go to school next year, and if I have a low-paying job I will need a loan to continue. Neither of these consequences is acceptable to me. Therefore, I will not stay on campus and study during spring vacation. (C, S, H, L, 1, P, G, N)

2. If Russia intervenes in Iran, then if the United States acts to protect its interests in the Middle East, either there will be confrontation between Russia and the United States or Israel to act as a surrogate for the United States. Israel will act as a surrogate if and only if it is absolutely assured of unlimited supplies of American weapons. If the United States meets this condition, however, the friendly Arab states will turn against the United States; the United States cannot allow that to happen. Therefore, if Russia intervenes in Iran and the United States acts to protect its interests in the Middle East, there will be a confrontation between the two superpowers. (R, U, C, 1, A, F)

3. If wages continue to rise, prices will also rise and people on fixed incomes will experience increasing hardship. If wages do not continue to rise, workers at the lower end of the pay scale will never be able to afford a decent life. Wages either will or will not continue to rise, so either people on fixed incomes win experience hardship or workers at the lower end of the pay scale win not be able to afford a decent life. (R, P, H, W)

4. Either I will take a trip to Europe this summer or I will save MY money and get married in September. If I do the latter, I will move to Denver. So if I don't go to Europe this summer I will move to Denver. (E, S, M, D)

5. If I buy a new car, I will be saddled with high monthly payments,, and if I buy a used car I will have high repair bills. I am unwilling to do either. Therefore, I will not buy a car. (N, M, U, R)

6. Either I will go to school for the next four years or I will be working for the next four years. If I go to school, I will forfeit the income that I could have been earning but will be prepared to do what I want to do. If I work, I will have the immediate but will lose the opportunity to have the career that I really want. I must choose, therefore, between an immediate income and the career that I really want. (S, W, I, C)

7. John's father is either an architect or a builder. If he is John's mother is an interior decorator and, a member of the city planning commission. If he is a builder, John's mother is either a school principal or a dentist. Therefore, if John's mother is not an interior decorator, then if she is not a school principal she is a dentist. (A, B, D, C, P, T)

H. Construct a formal proof of validity for the following (Halverson, p.198)

1. R ⊃ [P ⊃ (K v Z)]   /∴ R ⊃ {R & [P ⊃ (K v Z)]}

2. 1 (B & G) ⊃ (M & ~K)
   2 ~(M & ~K)   /∴ ~(B & G)

3. 1 [(K & L):) ⊃ (A v B)] & (D ⊃ (R & N)]
   2 (K & L) v D   /∴ (A v B) v (R & N)

4. (A v L) & R   /∴ [(A v L) & R] v K

5. 1 (A v B) ⊃ K
   2 (C v D) ⊃ L   /∴ [(A v B) ⊃ K] & [(C v D) ⊃ L]

6. 1 (M & R) v [B ⊃ (L v -N)]
   2 ~(M & R)   /∴B ⊃ (L v ~N)

7. 1 [(A v B) ⊃ E] & [(C v D) ⊃ F]
   2 (A v B) v (C v D)   /∴E v F

I. Deduce the conclusions of each of the following arguments from their premises (Gustason, p.83)

1. ~B
   [B v (~A v C)] & (A v B)
   ∴(~A v C) & (~B v C)

2. C&D
   ∴[C & (D v ~D)] v (E v ~E)

3. N v (S v -A)
   ~N & ~P
   ~ & ~Q
   ∴ ~N & (~S & ~A)

4. A v B
   ~A &C
   ∴ (B v ~D) & (D v ~D)

J. Derive a valid conclusion from each of the following premise sets. (Churchill, p. 267)

1. If Eric passed the bar exam, then he will practice law in Massachusetts. Eric passed the bar exam.

2. If Eric passed the bar exam, then he will practice law in Massachusetts. Eric will not practice law in Massachusetts.

3. Either Lisa will vacation in Puerto Rico or Cancun. Lisa will not vacation in Puerto Rico.

4. Either Lisa will vacation in Puerto Rico or Cancun. Lisa will not vacation in Cancun.

5 It's not true that both Derek and Glynda can place first in the competition. Derek will place first in the competition.

6. Derek and Glynda will not both place first in the competition. Glynda will place first in the competition.

7. If Robin helps Sarah, then Sarah will help Willard. If Sarah will help Willard, then Willard will help Albertine.

8. Nicholas enjoys the cinema. Nicholas enjoys art galleries.

9. Nicole will visit Montreal if and only if she has a friend at McGill University. Nicole will visit Montreal.

10. Nicole will visit Monteal just in case she has a friend at McGill University. Nicole does not have a friend at McGill University.

11. If Leonard is admitted to the University of Toronto, then he will attend college in Ontario. If Leonard is admitted to McMaster University, then he will attend college in Ontario. Either Leonard will be admitted to the University of Toronto or he will be admitted to McMaster University.

12. If Gloria is called as a witness, then she will commit perjury. If Renaldo is called as a witness, then his testimony will implicate Gloria. Either Gloria will not commit perjury or Renaldo's testimony will not implicate Gloria.

K The following symbolized arguments are substitution instances of valid argument forms. Identify the valid argument form for each substitution instance. (Churchill, p.267.)

1. (A & B) ≡ (B ⊃ C)   4. ~[G & (H ⊃ I)]
   (A & B)   (H ⊃ I)
   ∴B ⊃ C   ∴~G

42

2. ~[(C v D) & (D & E)]
   D & E
   ∴ ~(C v D)

5. (I & J) K
   K (I v L)
   ∴ (I & J) ⊃ (I v L)

3. (E & F)VG
   ~(E & F)
   ∴ G

6. J ⊃ (L v M)
   ~(L v M)
   ∴ ~J

L. Translate and construct proofs for each of the following. (Neidorff, p.133.)

   1. If the merchants are generous the drive will succeed. If the merchants are generous the solicitors will be well treated. The merchants are generous. Therefore, the drive will succeed and the solicitors will be well treated.

   2. The merchants are generous and the reporters not. The lawyers are generous and the doctors not. If the merchants are generous the drive will succeed, and if the lawyers are generous, legal obstacles can be overcome. If the legal obstacles can be overcome and the drive succeeds, the hospital will be built. So it will be built.

M. Make up an argument such that the deduction of its conclusion from its premises requires that each of our five rules be used at least twice. (Gustason, p.83.)

Chapter Seven

Rules of Replacement Part II, "Equivalencies (Partially Completed)

A. For the following deductions, indicate how each line following the premises was derived, and name the rule that justifies it. Both rules of implication and transformation rules may be employed. (Churchill, pp.283-284.)

1.
    1. (A v B) ⊃ C   Premise
    2. ~B ⊃ D   Premise
    3. ~D / ∴ C   Premise/Conclusion
    4. ~(~B)
    5. B
    6. B v A
    7. A v B
    8. C

2.
    1. (A&B) ⊃ C   Premise
    2. D ⊃ A   Premise
    3. A ⊃ (B ⊃ C) / ∴ (D & B) ⊃ C   Premise/Conclusion
    4. D ⊃ (B ⊃ C)
    5. (D & B) ⊃ C

3.
    1. P&Q   Premise
    2. ~(P & R)   Premise
    3. (~R V S) ⊃ T /∴ T   Premise/Conclusion
    4. P
    5. ~R
    6. ~R v S
    7. T

4.
    1. ~PVQ   Premise
    2. ~(Q & ~S) /∴ P ⊃ S   Premise/Conclusion
    3. P ⊃ Q
    4. Q ⊃ S
    5. P ⊃ S

5.
    1. A v (B & C)   Premise
    2. (A v B) ⊃ D /∴ D   Premise/Conclusion
    3. (A v B) & (A v C)
    4. A v B
    5. D

6. 1. (P v Q) v R   Premise
    2. ~P   Premise
    3. (Q v R) ⊃ (S & T) / ∴ T   Premise/Conclusion
    4. P v (Q v R)
    5. Q v R
    6. S &T
    7. T

7. 1. S ⊃ T   Premise
    2. (S & T) ⊃ U   Premise
    3. ~(S & U) / ∴ ~S   Premise/Conclusion
    4. S ⊃ (S & T)
    5. S ⊃U
    6. S ⊃ (S & U)
    7. ~S

8. 1. (P v ~Q) v R   Premise
    2. ~P v (Q & ~P) / ∴ Q ⊃ R   Premise/Conclusion
    3. (~P v Q) & (~P v P)
    4. ~P v ~P
    5. ~P
    6. P v (~Q v R)
    7. ~Q v R
    8. Q ⊃ R

9. 1. (H ⊃ I) ⊃ (~J ⊃ K)   Premise
    2. ~I ⊃ K   Premise
    3. H ⊃ ~K / ∴ J v K   Premise/Conclusion
    4. ~(~K) ⊃ ~H
    5. K ⊃ ~H
    6. ~I ⊃ ~H
    7. H ⊃ I
    8. ~J ⊃ K
    9. ~(~J) v K
    10. J v K

10.1. L ⊃ (M&N)   Premise
   2. 0 ⊃ P   Premise
   3. M ⊃ ~L   Premise
   4. ~0 ⊃ L   Premise
   5. ~P v [Q v (L v R)]   Premise
   6. Q ⊃ ~P / ∴ R   Premise/Conclusion
   7. ~L v (M & N)
   8. (~L v M) & (~L v N)
   9. ~L v M
   10. L ⊃ M
   11. L ⊃ ~L
   12. ~L v -L
   13. ~L
   14. ~(~O)
   15. 0
   16. P
   17. ~(~P)
   18. Q v (L v R)
   19. (Q v L) v R
   20. ~Q
   21. ~Q & ~L
   22. ~(Q V L)
   23. R

B. In each of the following deductions the first two lines are premises. State the justification for each of the other lines that are not premises. (Barker, pp.98-99.)

1. 1. A ⊃ B
   2. C ⊃ A
   3. C ⊃ B
   4. ~B ⊃ ~C

2. 1. B v (A & ~C)
   2. ~B
   3. A & ~C
   4. ~C

3. 1. A & B
   2. B ⊃ C
   3. B
   4. C

4. 1. (E & F) & D
   2. (E & F) ⊃ H
   3. E & F
   4. H

5. 1. C ⊃ A
   2. ~(A & B)
   3. ~A v ~B
   4. A ⊃ ~B
   5. C ⊃ ~B

6. 1. (E v F) ⊃ (A & B)
   2. ~(A & B)
   3. ~(E v F)
   4. ~E & ~F
   5. ~F

7. 1. G ⊃ ~H
   2. ~G ⊃ K
   3. G v ~G
   4. ~H v K
   5. H ⊃ K

8. 1. K v (C ⊃ K)
   2. ~K
   3. C ⊃ K
   4. ~C
   5. ~C & ~K

9. 1. (A ⊃ B) & (C ⊃ D)
   2. ~B v ~D
   3. ~A v ~C
   4. ~C v ~A
   5. C ⊃ ~A

10.1. H ⊃ J
   2. H
   3. J
   4. J ⊃ (J v K)
   5. J v K

C. Stated below are ten valid arguments, each followed by a formal proof of validity. Justify each statement in the proof by reference to the appropriate preceding statement or statements and the appropriate elementary valid argument form or replacement rule.

1. 1. A ⊃ (B ⊃ ~C)
    2. A & B / ∴ C ⊃ D
    3. (A & B) ⊃ ~C
    4. ~C
    5. ~C v D
    6. C ⊃ D

2. 1. A V [B ⊃ (C ⊃ D)
    2. ~A /∴ C ⊃ (B ⊃ D)
    3. B ⊃ (C ⊃ D)
    4. (B & C) ⊃ D
    5. (C ⊃ B) ⊃ D
    6. C ⊃ (B ⊃ D)

3. 1. V ≡ (X ⊃ Y)
    2. V / ∴ X ⊃ (Y v Z)
    3. [V ⊃ (X ⊃ Y)] & [(X ⊃ Y) ⊃ V]
    4. V ⊃ (X ⊃ Y)
    5. X ⊃ Y
    6. (X ⊃ Y) v Z
    7. (~X v Y) v Z
    8. ~X v (Y v Z)
    9. X ⊃ (Yv Z)

4. 1. K ⊃ (L v M)
    2. K & ~L/ ∴ R ⊃ M
    3. K
    4. L v M
    5. ~L
    6. M
    7. M v ~R
    8. ~R v M
    9. R ⊃ M

5. 1. A ⊃ (B & C)
    2. ~B / ∴ ~A
    3. ~A v (B & C)
    4. (~A v B) & (~A v C)
    5. ~A v B
    6. ~A

48

6. 1. K ⊃ [L ⊃ (M & N)]
    2. K / ∴ (L ⊃ M) & (L ⊃ N)
    3. L ⊃ (M & N)
    4. ~L v (M & N)
    5. (~L v M) & (~L v N)
    6. (~L v M) & (L ⊃ N)
    7. (L ⊃ M) & (L ⊃ N)

7. 1. K ⊃ (L & M)
    2. N ⊃ (~L v ~M)
    3. (N ⊃ R) & (K v O) / ∴ O
    4. N & R
    5. N
    6. ~L v ~M
    7. ~(L & M)
    8. ~K
    9. K v O
    10. O

8. 1. (M v R) ⊃ (P ⊃ X)
    2. M & P / ∴ (P & Q) ⊃ X
    3. M
    4. M v R
    5. P ⊃ X
    6. ~P v X
    7. (~P v X) v ~Q
    8. ~Q v (~P v X)
    9. (~Q v P) v X
    10. ~(Q & P) v X
    11. (Q & P) ⊃ X
    12. (P & Q) ⊃X

9. 1. ~A v [B ⊃ (C & D)]
    2. A/ ∴ B ⊃ D
    3. A ⊃ [B ⊃ (C & D)]
    4. B ⊃ (C & D)
    5. ~B v (C & D)
    6. (~B v C) & (~B v D)
    7. ~B v D
    8. B ⊃D

10.1. A v [(B v Q) ⊃ D]
  2. ~A / ∴ C ⊃ D
  3. (B v C) ⊃ D
  4. ~D ⊃ ~(B v C)
  5. ~D ⊃ (~B & ~C)
  6. ~~D v (~B & ~C)
  7. D v (~B & ~C)
  8. (D v ~B) & (D v ~C)
  9. D v ~C
  10. ~C v D
  11. C ⊃ D

50

Chapter Eight

Rules of Replacement Part II, "Equivalencies"

A. In each of the following arguments, the conclusion is derivable from the premises using both inference rules and rules of replacement. Complete each derivation. (McKay, p.120)

   1. 1. A v (B & C)
      2. D ⊃ ~(B & C)
      3. D / ∴ A

   2. 1. A ⊃ B
      2. B ⊃ (C v E)
      3. [A ⊃ (C v E)] ⊃ (D v F) / ∴ D v F

   3. 1. B ⊃ (C v D)
      2. ~C
      3. B / ∴ D

   4. 1. A ⊃ B
      2. (C & D) v A
      3. (C & D) ⊃ E
      4. (E v B) ⊃ F / ∴ F

   5. 1. (A ⊃ B) v C
      2. D ⊃ E
      3. ~C / ∴ B v E

B. In each of the following arguments, the conclusion is derivable with just three applications of the inference rules. (You may need to use rules of replacement as well.) Complete each derivation. (McKay, p.120)

   1. 1. A ⊃ E
      2. E ⊃ C
      3. A / ∴ A & C

   2. 1. (B v A) ⊃ E
      2. E (A & C)
      3. A / ∴ A & C

3. 1. (B v A) ⊃ (E & C)
   2. C ⊃ B
   3. C v D
   4. D ⊃ A /∴ C

4. 1. A ⊃ (C v D)
   2. A ⊃ ~C
   3. A /∴ A & C

5. 1. A ⊃ B
   2. A v C
   3. ~B /∴ C & ~A

6. 1. B ⊃ ~D
   2. A
   3. C ⊃ E
   4. (B v A) ⊃ (B ⊃ C) /∴ ~D v E

C. Each of the following arguments is an instance of one of the valid argument forms included in the system of rules developed in this chapter. In each case, identify the rule. (McKay, p.119.)

1. 1. (A v B) ⊃ C
   2. D ⊃ (A v B) /∴ D ⊃ C

2. 1. A & ~(B & C) /∴ C v [A & ~ (B &C)]

3. 1. ~(A v B)
   2. (C & D) ⊃ (A v B) /∴ ~(C & D)

4. 1. ~(A & B) v (C & D)
   2. ~(C & D) /∴ ~(A & B)

5. 1. (A v B) ⊃ C
   2. (A v B) v D
   3. D ⊃ (E & F) /∴ C v (E & F)

D. Show that each of the following is valid. (McKay, p.134.)

1. 1. A ⊃ B
   2. ~C ⊃ D
   3. ~(B & C) /∴ D v ~A

2. 1. (A & B) ⊃ (C v D)
   2. (E & B) ⊃ A /∴ (E & B) ⊃ (C v D)

52

3. 1. B ≡ (C & A)
   2. C ⊃ ~A / ∴ ~B

4. 1. (A & B) ⊃ (~D ⊃ ~C)
   2. F ⊃ A / ∴ (F & C) ⊃ (D v ~B)

5. 1. (B & C) ≡ (A v D)
   2. C & ~A / ∴ B ≡ D

6. 1. A ⊃ (B ≡ C)
   2. B & ~C
   3. ~A ⊃ D / ∴ D

E. Prove that the following arguments are valid. (Churchill, p.285.)

(1) (A & B) ⊃ C
   ~A v B
   A / ∴ C

(2) A ⊃ B
   C ⊃ D
   ~A ⊃ F
   ~F / ∴ B v D

(3) (C & D) ⊃ F
   G ⊃ C / ∴ (G & D) ⊃ F

(4) (C ⊃ D) & (F ⊃ G)
   C v F
   (D v G) ⊃ H / ∴ H

(5) (P ⊃ Q) ⊃ (R & S)
   (R & S) ⊃ (T ≡ W)
   ~(T ≡ W) / ∴ ~(P ⊃ Q)

(6) P ≡ Q
   Q ⊃ R / ∴ (~P v R) & (~Q v P)

(7) A v (B & C)
   (A ⊃ B) & (C ⊃ D)
   ~D & ~E / ∴ B

(8) (A ⊃ B) & (A v C)
    (C ⊃ D) & (C v A) / ∴ B v D

(9) D ⊃ C
    E ⊃ F
    (C v F) ⊃ G
    ~G / ∴ ~(D v E)

(10) ~(P & Q)
     Q v (R ⊃ S)
     P & ~S / ∴ R ⊃ (R & D)

(11) R & S
     (R v T) ⊃ (R ⊃ U)
     S ⊃ V / ∴ U & V

(12) L ⊃ M
     (N v 0) ⊃ L
     (~L v M) ⊃ 0 / ∴ M

(13) L & ~M
     [(L v N) & ~M] ⊃ (N & ~O)
     P ⊃ O
     N v P / ∴ N & ~P

(14) ~(Q ⊃ R)
     Q ⊃ S
     T ⊃ R / ∴ ~(S ⊃ T)

F. Each is valid by the method of formal deduction. (Churchill, pp.285-286.)

1. If Gail takes either precalculus or business mathematics, then she will have met the requirements for graduation. So, if she takes business mathematics, she will have met the requirements for graduation. (P, B, R)

2. If the country is in a state of anarchy, it cannot be reformed unless a charismatic leader appears. No charismatic leader can appear if the country is in a state of anarchy. The country surely is in a state of anarchy. Hence, it cannot be reformed. (A, R, C)

3. Either Michael will go to law school, or he will study forestry if he works as a park ranger. If I know him, he will not study forestry. Consequently, if he works as a park ranger, he will also go to law school. (L, F, R)

4. Wilkins would have won the case if Jenkins turned state's evidence, provided that Jenkins could be located in time. Although Wilkins didn't win, Jenkins was found in time. Thus, Jenkins didn't turn state's evidence. (W, S, L)

5. Either the president is mistaken or the senator is telling the truth. If the senator is telling the truth, then either the president's press secretary is lying or the White House chief of staff is suppressing evidence. The president is not mistaken and the press secretary is not lying. Thus, the chief of staff is suppressing evidence. (M, T, L, S)

6. If the guerrillas' demands are met, then international terrorism will increase. On the other hand, if the guerrillas' demands are not met, innocent hostages will suffer. So either international terrorism will increase or innocent hostages will suffer. (D, T, H)

7. It's not the case both that the senator will be elected and that he will not campaign in New York State. If he campaigns in New York State, then he must campaign vigorously for both black and Jewish votes. He will not campaign vigorously for Jewish votes. Therefore, the senator will not be elected. (E, C, B, 1)

8. If it is the case that Edith either went to the Bar Association meeting in Boston or went to Cape Cod for the week, then she left the Brewster case unprepared. If she didn't finish her work on the Brewster case, then she didn't finish the Dillon case. But if she has left the latter case unprepared, shell surely return on Saturday. Edith did go to the Bar Association meeting. So, she will return on Saturday. (M, C, B, D, S)

9. Either the federal government won't cut welfare programs, or poor blacks will riot if big business prospers. If poor blacks do riot, then the federal government won't cut welfare programs. But it won't happen that both big business will prosper and the federal government won't cut welfare programs. Therefore, either big business won't prosper or poor blacks won't riot. (W, R, B)

10. If the United States increases defense spending, then American leaders won't be intimidated by the Soviet military buildup. But Soviet leaders will be intimidated if the United States increases defense spending. If the Soviet leaders are intimidated, they are sure to increase the deployment of Warsaw Pact troops in Eastern Europe and intimidate American leaders after all. Thus, increasing defense spending in the United States is a sufficient condition for the intimidation of American leaders. (D, 1, S, W)

11. Either India will implement birth control programs and avert mass starvation, or birth control will be implemented and martial law will be declared. Mass starvation will not be averted; and if birth control is implemented, a popular uprising will occur. Thus, a popular uprising will occur. (1, A, M, P)

12. If the Soviets are bargaining in good faith and they are not on the verge of a technological breakthrough, then a new treaty will be negotiated with them. If the Soviets are not on the verge of a technological breakthrough and United States intelligence is reliable, a new treaty will be negotiated, and then the United States will cut back on defense spending. The United States will not cut back on defense spending. Furthermore, either the Soviets are on the verge of a technological breakthrough or United States intelligence is unreliable, or the Soviets are not bargaining in good faith. Therefore, no new treaty will be negotiated with them. (S, V, T, 1, D)

13. Either Hartley cheated on his logic exam, or he did not cheat and he failed. If he failed, he will be depressed. If he cheated, he will be depressed only if he is ashamed of himself. Hartley is not ashamed of himself, but he is depressed. Therefore, he failed and he did not cheat. (C, F, D, A)

14. If I do these logic deductions, then I won't have time left to read Moby Dick. I can get an A in English only if I read Moby Dick, and I'll be miserable unless I get an A in English. But if I don't finish these logic deductions, I'll be too distracted to concentrate on Moby Dick, and without concentration on Moby Dick, I can't get an A in English. Either I do these deductions or I do not. So I won't get an A in English. (D, R, E, M, C)

15. If God is omnipotent, then he can do anything, If he is omniscient, then he knows that evil exists. If he knows that evil exists and can do anything, then he would eradicate evil if he was also beneficent. But evil continues unabated in the world. Therefore, either God is not omniscient, or if he can do anything, he is not beneficent. (Op, D, Os, K, E, B)

G. Construct completely detailed proofs for the following arguments. (Neidorf, pp. 148-149.)

1. Either the apples or pears are ripe. The pears are not ripe. Hence, the melons or apples are ripe.

2. The melons, pears and apples, and cucumbers are ready. If the cucumbers and pears are ready, we can make a market trip today. Hence, we can make a market trip today.

3. If the trees are tall, the wind will not blow through. If the trees are strong, the ground will not erode. The trees are tall or strong. Therefore, the trees will need further cutting or the ground will not erode or the wind will not blow through.

4. The trees are tall or strong or resistant to cold or heavily leafed. They are not resistant to cold, nor tall, nor heavily leafed. Hence, they are strong.

5. What reasonable premise makes the following valid? "If he is kindly to children, he will help us. If he is inordinately cruel he will actively hinder us and prevent our helping. If he prevents our helping and actively hinders us, or he helps us, then we shall have to punish him or reward him. Hence, we shall indeed have to reward or punish him."

6. What significant conclusion can be inferred from the following? "If the president fails to act, then if the banks fail there will be a lack of currency. If the courts take a hand, then if appeals are made money will be released. Either the president will fail to act or the courts will take a hand. If there is a lack of currency there will be a serious depression. It is not the case that money will be released when appeals are made."

I. The following arguments are all valid. Construct two proofs for each, one using the principle of material substitution and one without it. (Neidorf, p.171.)

1. The jury will acquit if and only if the judge uses our proposed instructions. The judge will use our proposed instructions if and only if he remembers that I went to Yale, too. Hence, the jury will acquit if and only if the judge remembers that I went to Yale, too.

2. The jury will acquit or recommend leniency. The jury will recommend leniency if and only if the judge encourages them. Hence, the jury will acquit or the judge will encourage them to recommend leniency.

3. Either you install a gold tooth or you install a plastic one and use inferior cement. You run the risk of losing the tooth if and only if you use inferior cement. Hence, you install a gold tooth unless you install a plastic one and run the risk of losing the tooth.

4. Either gold fillings are dependable or silver fillings may be used. If special cements are employed or gold fillings are dependable; and if furthermore he works carefully and silver fillings may be used, or he is very experienced; then it would be right to let him do the work. He is very experienced, or he works carefully and special cements are employed. If special cements are employed the objections to silver can be met. Silver fillings may be used if the objections to silver can be met. If silver fillings can be used special cements are also employed. Therefore, it would be right to let him do the work.

J. Construct deductions to establish validity. (Barker, p.99-100.)

1. ~K & ~J, K v H, ∴ H
2. J & K, ~(K & H) / ∴ ~H
3. ~E v F, G ⊃ E / ∴ G ⊃ F
4. A & D, C v C / ∴ D & C
5. C ⊃ D, ~D ⊃ D, ∴ D
6. J, A ⊃ K, ~(K & J), ∴ ~A
7. ~H v J, ~J v ~J, ∴ ~H
8. A ⊃ B, A ⊃ ~B, ∴ ~A
9. J ⊃ K, ~(H & ~H) ⊃ ~K, ∴ ~J
10. A, C ⊃ D, ~(D & A), ∴ ~C

11. E ⊃ J, ~J ⊃ ~H, ~(~H & ~E), ∴ J
12. B ⊃ (A & ~A), C ⊃ B, ∴ ~C
13. ~A ⊃ D, B v B, ~D, ∴ (B & A) v (B & D)
14. (K v ~K) ⊃ ~J, (E & F) ⊃ J, ∴ ~E v ~F
15. G ⊃ (K & J), ~(H v H), (U & K) ⊃ H, ∴ ~G
16. ~C ⊃ ~D, C ⊃ D, ~C ⊃ ~A, C ⊃ A, ∴ D ≡ A
17. ~(D v ~E) ≡ ~F, F, ∴ E ⊃ (D v G)
18. H & H, K ⊃ ~K, ~(G & H), ∴ ~(G v K)
19. E ⊃ D, ~B ⊃ ~D, B ≡ ~A, ∴ E ⊃ A
20. (E & F) ⊃ G, H ⊃ E, ∴ F ⊃ (H ⊃ G)

K. Symbolize each argument using the suggested letters. Then construct a deduction to show that it is valid. (Barker, p.100.)

1. If the patient had no fever, then malaria was not the cause of his illness. But malaria or food poisoning was the cause of his illness. The patient had no fever. Therefore, food poisoning must have caused his illness. (F, M, P)

2. The centrifuge is to be started if the specimen remains homogenous. Either the specimen remains homogeneous, or a white solid is precipitated. A white solid is not being precipitated. So the centrifuge is to be started. (C' S. W)

3. Had Franklin D. Roosevelt been a socialist, he would have been willing to nationalize industries. Had he been willing to nationalize industries, this would have been done during the Depression. But no industries were nationalized during the Depression. Hence Roosevelt must not have been a socialist. (R, W, D)

4. If either the husband or the wife paid the premium that was due, then the policy was in force and the cost of the accident was covered. If the cost of the accident was covered, they were not forced into bankruptcy. But they were forced into bankruptcy. Therefore, the husband did not pay the premium that was due. (H, W, P, C, B)

L. Deduce the conclusions of each of the following arguments from their premises. (Gustason, p.102.)

1. 1. (D ⊃ C) & (A ⊃ B)
   2. C & A / ∴ B v D

2. 1. ~(A & ~R)
   2. ~(R & S) / ∴ S ⊃ ~A

3. 1. (R ⊃ S) v T
   2. ~(S v T) / ∴ ~R v ~Q

4. 1. L ⊃ N
   2. (~N ⊃ ~L) ⊃ (M ⊃ P)
   3. ~P / ∴ ~M

5. 1. A
   2. B / ∴ B ≡ A

6. 1. S ⊃ (M ⊃ W)
   2. P ⊃ (M & S) / ~P v W

7. 1. A v ~L
   2. C v L / ∴ A v ~C

8. 1. ~E v (~W v ~A)
   2. (W & A) v (~W & ~A) / ∴ ~E v (~W & ~A)

9. 1. (Z & M) ⊃ (S v A)
   2. Z ⊃ ~S / ∴ (Z & ~A) ⊃ ~M

10. 1. K ≡ Q
    2. (K & V) ≡ ~(Q v V) / ∴ K ⊃ ~V

M. Symbolize each of the following arguments; then deduce their conclusions from their premises. (Gustason, pp.102-103.)

1. The number 91 is prime just in case it is not composite. The number 91 is not both prime and divisible by 7. The number 91 is divisible by 7. Therefore the number 91 is composite. (P, C, D)

2. I'm damned if I do, and damned if I don't. Therefore I'm damned. (M, D)

3. If argument (1) is sound then it is valid. If argument (1) is sound then its premises are true. Therefore if argument (1) is sound, then it is valid and its premises are true. (S, V, P)

4. If argument (1) is sound, then it is valid and its premises are true. Thus, if argument (1) is sound then it is valid, and if argument (1) is sound then its premises are true. (S, V, P)

5. If the President sounds optimistic then the stock market will go up. So if the economic news is bad but the President sounds optimistic, the stock market will go up. (0, U, B)

6. The runner on first base will break with the pitch, but the runner on third will score only if the catcher throws to second. The catcher will not throw to second if the runner on first breaks with the pitch. Therefore the runner on third will not score. (F, T, S)

7. If the front of a bicycle clunks on rough roads, either its front wheel isn't tight or its headset is loose. So if its front wheel is tight, then if a bicycle clunks on rough roads, its headset is loose. (B, F, H)

8. If my partner's lead of the queen of hearts was not a mistake, then he has either the heart king or the heartjack as well. If he has the heart king, then he made a mistake when he failed to respond to my opening bid. So if my partner made no mistake when he failed to respond to my opening bid and made no mistake either in leading the queen of hearts, he has the heart jack. (Q, K, J, B)

9. If God can create a stone too heavy for Him to lift, then there is something God cannot do. If it is not the case that God can create a stone too heavy for Him to lift, then there is something God cannot create. If there is something God cannot do then God is not omnipotent, and if there is something He cannot create then He is not omnipotent. Therefore God is not omnipotent. (S, D, C, O)

10. If my plans are going to work out, then I'm going to get a D on the first test but go into the final with a high average. If I study fairly hard but skip the hard problems, then I'll get a B on the second test. If I get a B on the second test but a D on the first, I won't go into the final with a high average. Therefore if I study fairly hard, then if I skip the hard problems my plans are not going to work out. (P, D, H, F, S, B)

11. If the price of the stock rises we'll make money on the shares we own, and if the price of the stock falls we'll make money on warrants we sold short. So if the price of the stock either rises or falls, we'll make money on either the shares we own or the warrants we sold short. (R, S, F, W)

12. The set of prime numbers is either denumerable or countable. If the set of prime numbers is countable, then it is either finite or denumerable. The set of prime numbers is not finite. it follows, then, that the set of prime numbers is denumerable. (D, C, F)

13. White will lose his bishop unless he moves his king. Black will either check with his queen or mate with his pawn. If White loses his bishop or Black checks with his queen, White will move his king and Black will mate with his pawn. Consequently, White will move his king and Black will mate with his pawn. (B. K, Q, P)

N. All of the arguments stated below are valid. Construct a formal proof of validity for each. (Halverson, pp.211-212.)

1. 1. (A & B) ⊃ C
   2. ~C / ∴ ~A V ~B

2. 1. (M v O) ⊃ R
   2. ~R / ∴ ~M

3. 1. (~M v P) v R
   2. M / ∴ P v R

4. 1. X ⊃ ~(R & ~Z)
   2. X / ∴ R ⊃ Z

5. 1. K ⊃ (L ⊃ M)
   2. ~M / ∴K v ~L

6. 1. Z ≡ L
   2. ~L / ∴ ~Z v R

7. 1. (R ⊃ K) & (~R ⊃ Z)
   2. ~K / ∴ Z

8. 1. R v (L & Z)
   2. ~Z / ∴ R

9. 1. (L & M) ⊃ K
   2. ~K / ∴ ~(M & L)

10. 1. (L v R) ⊃ Q
    2. (Q ⊃ E) & ~E / ∴ ~R

11. 1. (B v S) ⊃ (K ≡ L)
    2. K & ~L / ∴ ~B

12. 1. D ⊃ ~(E v F)
    2. (E v F) & (~D ⊃ R) / ∴ R

13. 1. (G ⊃ K) v ~(L & M)
    2. G & ~K / ∴ ~L v ~M

14. 1. L ⊃ (R ⊃ Z)
    2. (Z ⊃ K) & ~K / ∴ R ⊃ ~L

15. 1. (A ⊃ B) & (C ⊃ B)
    2. ~B / ∴ ~A & ~C

16. 1. (A ≡ B) ⊃ ~L
    2. (A ⊃ B) & (B ⊃ A) / ∴L ⊃ K

17. 1. Z ⊃ (L ⊃R)
    2. (L v K) & ~K / ∴ Z ⊃ R

18.1. Z ⊃ [(S v L) ⊃ M]
   2. (~B v Z) & B / ∴ S ⊃ M

19.1. G ≡ [(A v B) ⊃ R]
   2. G / ∴ B ⊃ R

20.1. ~A v [(K ⊃ L) & (R ⊃ L)]
   2. A / ∴ (K V R) ⊃ L

O. Construct a proof for each of the following. Any of the rules may be employed and there are no invalid arguments. Supposing the premises are inconsistent, what problems does this raise? Check for consistency of the premises. (Manicus and Kruger, p. 124)

1. 1. (p V q) ⊃ rs
   2. r ⊃ t
   3. ~ts / ∴ ~p

2. 1. (p ⊃ q)
   2. ~(r V s) / ∴ p

3. 1. (pq V rs)
   2. p ⊃ ~p / ∴ r

4. 1. (p ⊃ q) ⊃ s
   2. (s V t) ⊃ pq
   3. s / ∴ r

5. 1. (p ⊃ q) (r ⊃ s)
   2. p(r V ~t) / ∴ q V s

6. 1. p ≡ q
   2. p V q / ∴ p

7. 1. (p ⊃ q)(r ⊃ s)
   2. (q ⊃ t)(s ⊃ u)
   3. t ⊃ ~u
   4. p ⊃ r / ∴ ~p

8. 1. (pq ⊃ r) p
   2. p ~q ⊃ ~r / ∴ q ≡ r

9. 1. ~pq ⊃ r
   2. ~(q ⊃ p)
   3. (r ⊃ s)(r ⊃ p) / ∴ s V q

10. 1. p ⊃ (q ⊃ r)
    2. ~s V p
    3. (q ⊃ r) ⊃ tu
    4. s / ∴ u V m

P. Construct proofs for the following, keeping in mind that some of them may be invalid. (Klein)

1. [(p ≡ q) ⊃ (r & t)] V ~q
   r & s
   u V ~(p V ~r)
   ∴ s ≡ t

2. (p ⊃ q) & (s ⊃ r)
   ~q V ~r
   ∴ s V z

Q. What is the most fundamental difference between the Rules of Inference and the Rules of Replacement? (Klein)

Chapter Nine

Conditional Proofs

A. Explain the concept of conditional proof. (Halverson, p.218.)

B. Justify each step in the following proofs. (Halverson, pp.218-219.)

1. 1. (A ⊃ K) & (L ⊃ R)
   2. (A v L) & ~K
   3. (R ⊃ M) / ∴ L ⊃ M
   4. L
   5. L ⊃ R
   6. R
   7. M
   8. L ⊃ M

2. 1. R ⊃ (L ⊃ Z)
   2. (L v M) & ~M / ∴ R ⊃ Z
   3. R
   4. L ⊃ Z
   5. L v M
   6. ~M
   7. L
   8. Z
   9. R ⊃ Z

3. 1. L ⊃ (~B v ~C)
   2. M ⊃ (B & C) / ∴ L ⊃ ~M
   3. L
   4. ~B v ~C
   5. ~(B & C)
   6. ~M
   7. L ⊃ ~M

4. 1. L v (X & ~Z)
   2. (L v X) ⊃ (Y v ~Z) / ∴ Z ⊃ Y
   ◄3. Z
   [4. L v X
   [5. Y v ~Z
   ►6. Y
   7. Z ⊃ Y

5. 1. A ⊃ [B ⊃ (C v D)]
   2. ~D / ∴ ~C ⊃ (~A v ~B)
   3. (A & B) ⊃ (C v D)
   ◄4. A & B
   [5. C v D
   ►6. C
   7. (A & B) ⊃ C
   8. ~C ⊃ ~(A & B)
   9. ~C ⊃ (~A v ~B)

C. Derive the conclusions from the premises. (Use Conditional Proof.) (McKay, p.143.)

1. A ⊃ C
   ∴(A & B) ⊃ C

2. (A ⊃ C) & (B ⊃ C)
   ∴ (A v B) ⊃ C

3. I ⊃ (M ⊃ H)
   ~H
   ∴ I ⊃ ~M

4. A v (B & C)
   C ⊃ ~A
   ∴ C ⊃ B

5. (H & ~J) C
   C ⊃ E
   ∴~J

6. ~(B & ~D)
   ~A ⊃ B
   C ⊃ (A ⊃ D)
   ∴ C ⊃ D

7. A ⊃ (B & D)
   B ⊃ (C v ~D)
   ~C v (B & E)
   ∴ A ⊃ (C & E)

8. A ⊃ [B v (C & D)]
   E ⊃ ~C
   B ⊃ (E & C)
   ∴ A ⊃ D

9. A ⊃ (B v C)
   A ⊃ ~C
   (A & B) ⊃ D
   ∴ A ⊃ D

10. A ⊃ B
    ~(D v A) ⊃ C
    ∴ ~(B v C) ⊃ (D & ~A)

11. ~[A & (B v C)]
    D ⊃ B
    E v C
    ∴ A ⊃ (E & ~D)

12. B ⊃ (D & ~D)
    (C & A) ⊃ ~E
    F ⊃ (D v E)
    ∴ A ⊃ (B ~F)

D. Construct deductions for the following, using CP when helpful. (Gustason, p.110.)

1. Jones has not learned how to use correctly the expression "Smith acted of his own free will" unless he has seen Smith acting freely and heard others use the expression "Smith is acting of his own free will." If all of our actions are determined according to physical laws, then no one ever acts of his own free will and Jones has never seen Smith acting freely. So if Jones has learned how to use correctly the expression "Smith acted of his own free will," not all of our actions are determined according to physical laws. (L, S, H, D, N)

2. If argument (1) has a false premise, it is unsound. If argument (1) is invalid, it is unsound. So if argument (1) either has a false premise or is invalid, then it is unsound. (F, S, V)

3. If argument (1) either has a false premise or is invalid, it is unsound. Consequently, if argument (1) has a false premise it is unsound and if argument (1) is invalid it is unsound. (F, V, S)

4. If government borrowing increases, then if the central banks monetize the debt, inflation will worsen. Therefore if government borrowing increases only if the central banks monetize the debt, then if government borrowing increases, inflation will worsen. (B, M, I)

5. If either Al's claim or Bill's claim is true, then Al's claim is true if and only if Bill's claim is true. It follows that Al's claim is true if and only if Bill's is. (A, B)

6. If Yossarian flies his missions, then if knowingly placing one's life in danger is irrational, then Yossarian is irrational. If Yossarian asks to be grounded and a request to avoid a perilous situation is rational, then Yossarian is rational. A request to avoid a perilous situation is rational if and only if knowingly placing one's life in danger is irrational. Therefore, if Yossarian flies his missions but asks to be grounded, then knowingly placing one's life in danger is rational and a request to avoid a perilous situation is irrational. (F, K, R, G, A)

E. Construct a formal proof of validity for each of the following arguments using a Conditional Proof at least once in the course of each proof. (Halverson, p. 220.)

  1. 1. (A ⊃ B) & [B ⊃ (~J & K)]
     2. J / ∴ A ⊃ ~K

  2. 1. (J ⊃ K) & (~J ⊃ R)
     2. R ⊃ X / ∴ ~K ⊃ X

  3. 1. B ⊃ (R v W)
     2. ~R / ∴ ~W ⊃ ~B

  4. 1. C ≡ (D v E)
     2. ~D / ∴ E v ~C

  5. 1. (B v W) (L v F)
     2. ~L / ∴ F v ~(B v W)

  6. 1. A v (B v C)
     2. ~C / ∴ ~B ⊃ A

  7. 1. (A & C) ⊃ ~B
     2. B v (K & L)
     3. A ⊃ C / ∴ ~K ⊃ (~A v ~C)

  8. 1. (L v K) & C
     2. ~B ⊃ ~(K & C)
     3. C ⊃ (L ⊃ ~S) / ∴ S ⊃ B

  9. 1. [(A v B) & C] ⊃ D
     2. (C ⊃ D) ⊃ (E ⊃ K)
     3. E / ∴ A ⊃ K

  10.1. [(P v Q) & R] ⊃ L
     2. (R ⊃ L) ⊃ (H ⊃ M)
     3. H / ∴ P ⊃ M

F. Construct conditional proofs for each of the following. (Manicas and Kruger, pp.129-130.)

  1. 1 p ⊃ q
     2 ~r ⊃ ~q   / ∴ p ⊃ r

  2. 1 (p V q) ⊃ rs
     2 (s V t) ⊃ u   / ∴ p ⊃ u

67

3. **1** $p \supset q$ $/ \therefore \sim(qr) \supset \sim(rp)$

4. **1** $p \supset (q \supset r)$
   2 $q \supset (r \supset s)$ $/ \therefore p \supset (q \supset s)$
   (Use conditionalization twice.)

5. **1** $pq \equiv r$
   2 $\sim r \supset (\sim p \lor s)$
   3 p $/ \therefore \sim s \supset pq$

6. If the cost of living rises, then interest rates increase and there are fewer housing starts. There are fewer housing starts or savings decrease only if investment opportunities are used up. Hence, if the cost of living rises, investment opportunities are used up. (p = the cost of living rises; q = interest rates increase; r = there are fewer housing starts; s = savings decrease; t = investment opportunities are used up.)

7. If the test subject asks for food, then he is hungry and if he is deprived of food for twenty-four hours, he is hungry, Analysis of the test subject's blood will indicate an absence of significant amounts of glucose only if he is deprived of food or asks for food. Hence, if the analysis of the subject's blood shows an absence of significant amounts of glucose, he is hungry. (p = subject asks for food; q = he is hungry; r = he is deprived of food; s = analysis shows an absence of glucose.)

8. If Jones carries Erie County, he must carry South Buffalo and the West Side. He'll carry South Buffalo only if there is a strong Irish vote for him. But if the Flanigan vote is strong and the voters don't turn out, then there won't be a strong Irish vote for Jones. Accordingly, if Jones carries Erie County, then if the Flanigan vote is strong, the voters turned out. (p = Jones carries Erie County; q = Jones carries South Buffalo; r = Jones carries the West Side; s = there is a strong Irish vote for Jones; t = the Flanigan vote is strong; u = the voters turn out.)

9. If sugar is put in water, then if it is water soluble, it dissolves. If it dissolves, then other conditions are under experimental control. But it is false that either other conditions are under experimental control or that the moon is made of green cheese. But if so, we must conclude that if sugar is water-soluble then it isn't put in water and it doesn't dissolve! (p = sugar is put in water; q = sugar is water-soluble; r = sugar dissolves; s = other conditions are under control; t = the moon is made of green cheese.)

9. Alphonse is the sort of guy who if he marries a beautiful woman, will be jealous and if he marries a rich woman, will be discontented. But if he is either jealous or discontented, he is not liberated. Moreover, if he marries a liberated woman, he'll be happy. Alphonse will marry either a beautiful woman, a rich woman, or a liberated woman. Hence, if he is liberated, he will be happy. (p = Alphonse marries a beautiful woman; q = he is jealous; r = he marries a rich woman; s = he is discontented; t = he is liberated; w = he marries a liberated woman; h = he is happy.)

Chapter Ten

Indirect Proofs

A. Explain the concept of a *Reduction Ad Absurdum* (RAA) proof. (Halverson, p.214.)

B. Justify each step in the following RAA proofs. (Halverson, pp.214-215.)

1. 1. (A ⊃ B) & (C ⊃ B)
   2. (A v C) & (B ⊃ D) / ∴ D
   3. ~ D
   4. B ⊃ D
   5. ~D ⊃ ~B
   6. ~B
   7. A v C
   8. B v B
   9. B
   10. B & ~B
   11. D

2. 1. (A ⊃ B) & (C ⊃ D)
   2. C v A
   3. (B v D) ⊃ R / ∴ R
   4. ~R
   5. ~R ⊃ ~(B v D)
   6. ~(B v D)
   7. A v C
   8. B v D
   9. (B v D) & ~(B v D)
   10. R

3. 1. X v (Y & Z)
   2. ~Z / ∴ X
   3. ~X
   4. Y & Z
   5. Z
   6. Z & ~Z
   7. X

4. 1. (A ⊃ N) & (L ⊃ M)
   2. A / ∴ N v M
   3. ~(N v M)
   4. ~N & ~M
   5. ~N
   6. A ⊃ N
   7. N
   8. N & ~N
   9. N v M

C. Deduce the conclusions of each of the following using the Indirect Proof procedure. (Gustason, p.114.)

1. A ⊃ E
  B F
  (E v F) ~G
  (G v H) ⊃ (A v B)
  ∴ ~G

2. (A v L) v O
  L ≡ O
  ∴ O v A

3. (R ⊃ S) & (F ⊃ W)
  ~(S v W)
  ∴ ~(F v R)

4. S
  ∴ (T ⊃ U) v (U ⊃ T)

5. A v (B & C)
  [D v (D ⊃ E)] ⊃ (A ⊃ C)
  ∴ C

6. [(A v B) & (C v D)] ⊃ E
  ∴ ~(A & D) v E

D. Derive the conclusion from the premises using the Indirect Proof method. (McKay, p.148.)

1. A v C
   C ⊃ D
   D ⊃ A
   ∴ A

2. ~A ⊃ (B v C)
   C v D
   ~B v ~D
   ∴ A v C

3. A ≡ B
   C ⊃ ~B
   C ⊃ A
   ∴ ~C

4. A ⊃ (D & E)
   C v E
   C ⊃ (A & ~D)
   ∴ E & ~C

5. A ⊃ (C & D)
   B ⊃ (E v ~C)
   E ⊃ (~A v ~D)
   ∴ ~(A & B)

6. (~A v B) ⊃ C
   A v ~D
   C ⊃ D
   ∴ A

7. B ⊃ (A & C)
   (A v ~C) ⊃ (B & C)
   ∴ A v C

8. ~A ⊃ (B ⊃ C)
   A v B
   B ⊃ ~C
   A ⊃ D
   ∴ A & D

E. Give *reductio ad absurdum* proofs of the following. (Manicas and Kruger, pp.133-134.)

1. 1 p ⊃ q
   2 ~(q V r)   / ∴ ~p

2. 1 (p ⊃ q)(r ⊃ q)
   2 s ⊃ (p V r)   / ∴ s ⊃ q

3. 1 p   / ∴ qr ⊃ p

4. 1 p ⊃ (q ⊃ r)
   2 p ⊃ q
   3 ~s ⊃ (r V p)   / ∴ s V r

5. 1 (p ⊃ q) ⊃ rs
   2 (r V t) (s ⊃ p)   / ∴ p

6. If Sam tries again, then neither George nor Ronald will cooperate. Ronald will cooperate. So Sam will try again only if George doesn't cooperate. (p = Sam tries again; q = George will cooperate; r = Ronald will cooperate.)

7. Sam will try again only if he is drafted at the convention. He won't be drafted at the convention unless the party supports him and not Ronald. If the party supports Sam, then it will support Ronald. Therefore, Sam will not try again. (p = Sam tries again; q = Sam is drafted at the convention; r = the party supports Sam; s = the party supports Ronald.)

8. If Gloria goes, then Sam will go. Sam will go only if Louie doesn't go; and if Red doesn't go, then Louie will. But either Gloria is going or Red isn't; so Gloria is going if and only if Louie isn't. (p = Gloria goes; q = Sam goes; r = Louie goes; s = Red goes.)

9. If either Jennifer or Harriet have dates, then if Julie is working, I won't be able to get a date. Julie is working; but if I am not able to get a date, I might as well go home for the weekend. So, if Jennifer has a date, f might as well go home for the weekend. (p = Jennifer has a date; q = Harriet has a date; r = Julie is working; s = I am able to get a date; t = I might as well go home for the weekend.)

10. If we are a rich nation, then we can help the poor. If we can help the poor, then surely we should. On the other hand, if the poor could help themselves, then we shouldn't help them. But if the poor can't help themselves, then there are not sufficient jobs. If there are not sufficient jobs, then we can't help the poor. But either the poor can help themselves or they cannot. Hence, either way, it seems that we are not a rich nation! (P = we are a rich nation; q = we can help the poor; r = we should help the poor; s = the poor can help themselves; t there are sufficient jobs.)

11. If liquidity preference remains constant and the supply of money increases, then the rate of interest falls. Either the marginal efficiency of capital does not decrease or best opportunities for investment are used up. During the period from July 1 to September 1, liquidity preference has remained constant. If the rate of interest falls, then the marginal efficiency of capital decreases. Hence, if the supply of money has increased from July 1 to September 1, then during that period, the best opportunities for investment were used up. (p = liquidity preference remained constant; q = the supply of money increased; r = the rate of interest falls; t = marginal efficiency of capital decreases; u = best opportunities for investment are used up.)

12. The right of free speech is a natural right if and only if each person in some sense possesses it and it is not a privilege given by a sovereign power. But if the right to free speech is a natural right, then the right to employment is also a natural right. If the right to employment is a natural right, then the right to free speech is not a privilege in the sense indicated. Still, free speech is a natural right only if every person possesses it equally, Hence if all persons possess the right to free speech then persons possess the right to free speech equally, or the right to employment is not a natural right. (p = the right to free speech is a natural right; q = each person possesses the right to free speech; r = the right to free speech is a privilege; s = the right to employment is a natural right; t = every person possesses the right to free speech equally.)

13. Either Marx was a Marxist or Lenin was a Bolshevik and Kautsky was Lenin's best friend. If Marx was a Marxist, then if Locke was a natural law theorist, Mill was a utilitarian. But if Marx was not a Marxist, then nobody was. Locke was a natural law theorist and Kautsky was anything but Lenin's best friend. Hence, either Mill was a utilitarian or nobody was a Marxist. (p = Marx was a Marxist; q = Lenin was a Bolshevik; r = Kautsky was Lenin's best friend; s = Locke was a natural law theorist; t = Mill was a utilitarian; u = nobody was a Marxist.)

Chapter Eleven

Conditional Proofs and/or Indirect Proofs

A. Using whatever methods seem most helpful, show that each of the following arguments is deductively valid. (Gustason, p.115.)

1. (C v D) ⊃ (C ⊃ B)
   (~A ⊃ B) ⊃ ~(D v E)
   ~C ⊃ D
   ∴ (A v B) ≡ C

2. A ⊃ B
   B ⊃ C
   ~A ⊃ ~C
   (~A & ~C) ⊃ F
   (A & C) ⊃ D
   ∴ D v F

3. A & ~A
   ∴ B

4. (F ⊃ S) & (R ⊃ W)
   F & R
   ∴ S & W

5. (E & W) ≡ (E & A)
   ∴ E ⊃ (W ≡ A)

6. D
   A ⊃ B
   E ⊃ C
   ~A ⊃ (D ⊃ E)
   (B v C) ⊃ F
   ∴ F

7. (A ⊃ B) ⊃ (B ⊃ D)
   O ⊃ (C ⊃ S)
   (~S ⊃ ~O) ⊃ A
   ∴ (A ⊃ B) ⊃ (~C v D)

8. ~A ⊃ [~A ⊃ (B & B)]
    B ⊃ [A ⊃ (C & ~C)]
    ∴ ~A ≡ B

9. [(D & C) v (~D & ~C)]
    (S v U)
    ~R ⊃ (D ⊃ C)
    ~D ⊃ ~C
    S ⊃ T
    ∴ (R ⊃ S) ⊃ (T v U)

10. (~~A v ~~B) ⊃ (D ⊃ ~L)
    (C ⊃ E) ⊃ [D & (L v ~A)]
    ∴ A ⊃ C

B. Symbolize the following arguments with the suggested letters, and prove that each argument is valid by using the indirect method. (Churchill, pp.289-290.)

1. General George Custer was defeated at the Battle of Little Big Horn. But he was defeated at this battle if and only if he was in Montana. If General Custer was in Wyoming, he was not in Montana. Therefore, he was not in Wyoming. (C, M, W)

2. If interest rates on bank loans increase, then mortgage money will become tighter and there will be fewer housing starts. There will be fewer housing starts only if personal income does not increase. Hence if interest rates on bank loans increase, personal income will fail to increase. (I, M, H, P)

3. If the professor is given tenure, then if his book is published and his teaching improves he will either be promoted or he will be given sabbatical leave. He will not be promoted and he will not be given sabbatical leave unless his book is published. His book is not going to be published, although his teaching has improved. Thus, if he is given tenure, then neither will he be promoted nor will he be given sabbatical leave. (T, B, I, P, S)

4. Either the assassination was the work of the mob, or else the crime was an inside job and the Secret Service is implicated. The mob could have committed the crime only if its assassins had precise information on the president's security. But the Secret Service is implicated if the mob had this information. Therefore, the Secret Service is definitely implicated. (M, J, S, P)

5. Either the coal strike will not be successful or coal miners' wage will rise. If wages do rise, then there will be an increase in the cost of making steel. It is not the case both that the cost of making steel will rise and the price of automobiles will not rise. If the price of automobiles does rise, then the cost-of-living index will rise. Therefore, if the coal strike is successful, the cost-of-living index will rise. (C, W, S, A, I)

75

C. Construct a formal proof for each of the following arguments. Use valid inferential forms, the conditional proof process, equivalence inferential forms, and indirect proof as needed. Should you become stuck with any of the first eight problems, there is a set of recipes following these problems. Before looking at the solutions, make a real effort, use the strategies and the goals appproach, and look for indirect proofs.

1. P ⊃ ~(N & B)
   (R v W) ⊃ C
   ∴ R

2. R v (W & F)
   (R v W) ⊃ C
   ∴ C

3. V ≡ S
   S
   ∴ V

4. I v ~H
   ∴ H ⊃ I

5. B ⊃ R
   R ⊃ ~B
   ∴ ~B

6. (~K v G) v C
   ∴ K ⊃ (G v C)

7. (A & I) v (A & S)
   ~Q
   ∴ D

8. G v W
   G v E
   ∴ G v (W & E)

9. U v (U v N)
   ∴ ~U ⊃ N

10. A ⊃ (S & Q)
    ~Q
    ∴ ~A

11. D v (O & P)
    ∴ D v P

12. (M & C) ⊃ I
    M & ~I
    ∴ ~C

13. M v ~A
    A
    ∴ M

14. F ⊃ N
    N ⊃ P
    ∴ ~F v P

15. ~V v U
    ~V v D
    (U & D) T
    ∴ V ⊃ T

16. (W v J) O
    ~O
    ∴ ~J

76

17. (R & W) v (R & F)
   ~W
   ∴ F

18. A ⊃ [(S & T) v O]
   [O v (S & T)] ⊃ R
   ∴ A ⊃ R

19. R ⊃ L
   L ⊃ J
   ~J v R
   ∴ R ≡ J

20. G v ~B
   ~(~G & B) ⊃ I
   ∴ I

21. R ⊃ K
   R ⊃ ~K
   ∴ ~R

22. U
   ~N
   ∴ ~(U N)

23. ~D v ~A
   D v ~H
   ∴ A ⊃ ~H

24. ~(M ⊃ T)
   (M & Q) & (~T ⊃ V)
   ∴ Q ⊃ V

25. W ⊃ (U ≡ G)
   ~G
   ∴ W ⊃ ~U

26. ~(A & R) ≡ ~C
   ~(C & O) ⊃ P
   ∴ ~A P

27. K ⊃ A
   ∴ (A & K) ≡ K

28. Z ⊃ [(K & A) ⊃ (L v T)]
   ~L & (L v A)
   ∴ Z ⊃ (K ⊃ T)

29. T ⊃ U
   ~(U & T)
   ~R ⊃ T
   ∴ R

30. J ⊃ (R ⊃ T)
   ~U ⊃ (R & V)
   (O v T) ⊃ S
   U v J
   ∴ U v S

77

D. Use the italicized letters for the required statement constants, and symbolize each of the following arguments. Next, construct a formal proof for each of them. If you become bogged down when attempting to construct formal proofs, be sure to review your symbolizations. All of the following are valid argumenst, but if you misymbolize them, you might wind up attempting to construct formal proofs for invalid arguments. (Wilson, p.184.)

1. Women either speak out against the male-dominated society, or they are treated like children. Women either speak out against the male-dominated society, or they are treated like servants. Hence, women either speak out against the male-dominated society, or they are either treated like children and servants.

2. Unless women receive equal pay, they aren't equal to men. Unless women receive equal respect, they aren't equal to men. So, only if women receive equal pay and equal respect, are they equal to men.

3. If either North Vietnam was defeated or South Vietnam continues to be an independent country, then the U.S. war effort in Vietnam was successful. The U.S. was effort in Vietnam wasn't successful. Hence, North Vietnam wasn't defeated.

4. If either the word 'broad' didn't originally mean "pregnant cow" or the word 'broad' isn't demeaning to women for other reasons, then it is acceptable to refer to women as "broads." It is not acceptable to refer to women as either "broads" or "chicks." So the word 'broad' originally meant "pregnant cow."

5. Unless criminals think about their crimes before committing them, capital punishment does not deter crime. If criminals think about their crimes before committing them and capital punishment deters crime, then capital punishment is justified. Capital punishment is justified only if it deters crime. Hence, capital punishment is justified if and only if it deters crime.

6. Unless we legalize drugs, we will have to spend more money on law enforcement, and a segment of our society will remain addicted to drugs. If we legalize drugs, then a segment of our society will continue using them; and, if a segment of our society continues using them, then a segment of our society will remain addicted to drugs. Consequently, a segment of our society will remain addicted to drugs.

E. Provide a formal proof for each of the following arguments. Use any of our inferential forms as needed. (Wilson, p.183.)

1. K v U
   ~K
   ∴ U

2. F ⊃ N
   N ⊃ P
   ∴ F ⊃ P

3. E ⊃ P
   R ⊃ L
   ∴ (E v R) ⊃ (P v L)

4. I ⊃ [(S & L) v P]
   (S & L) ⊃ C
   P ⊃ H
   ∴ I ⊃ (C v H)

5. ~A ⊃ (S & I)
   ~S
   ∴ A

6. ~M v ~S
   (R & B) ⊃ S
   M
   ∴ R ⊃ ~B

7. (K v P) & (K v A)
   (K v W) ≡ (M ⊃ C)
   ∴ ~(P & A) ⊃ ~(M & ~C)

8. (C v B) ⊃ T
   (~C & ~B) ⊃ O
   ~O v S
   ~T
   ∴ S

9. H ⊃ (K ⊃ C)
   Y ⊃ (D ⊃ S)
   (H v Y) & (K & D)
   ∴ C v S

10. Z ⊃ [(K & A) ⊃ (L v T)
    ~L &(L v A)
    ∴ Z ⊃ (K ⊃ T)

F. Using both the indirect method and the method of formal deduction, prove that each of the following arguments is valid. (Constuct two proofs for each argument.) (Churchill, p.289.)

1. A ⊃ B
   B ⊃ C
   D v ~C
   A
   ∴ D

2. D ⊃ E
   E ⊃ F
   F ⊃ G
   ∴ D G

3. ~A v B
   ~(B & ~C)
   ~C
   ∴ ~A

4. (~A v ~C) v B
   ~C ⊃ D
   E v ~D
   ~E & A
   ∴ B

5. A & (B ⊃ C)
   C ⊃ D
   ~(~B & A)
   ~D v (~E v F)
   ∴ E ⊃ F

G. Use the italicized letters for the required statement constants, and symbolize each of the following arguments. Next, construct a formal proof for each of them. (Gustason, p.116.)

1. If Watson sinks his thirty-foot putt, then if the spectators let out a spontaneous shout then Kite will miss his mere tap-in. If Watson sinks his thirty-foot putt only if Kite misses his tap-in, one of the two will be on the practice tee tonight. Therefore, if the spectators let out a spontaneous shout, or if Kite misses his tap-in, or if Watson does not sink his thirty-foot putt, then either Watson or Kite will be on the practice tee tonight.

2. Yossarin is crazy if he flies his missions, and is he is crazy then he is not obligated to fly his missions. However, if Yossarian asks to be grounded then he is showing concern for his own safety in the face of real, immediate danger, and if he shows such concern that his is *not* crazy and *is* obligated to fly his missions. Moreover, Yossarian won't fly his missions only if he both asks to be grounded and is not obligated to fly them. Therefore Yossarian is not obligated to fly his missions but flies them nonetheless.

3. If the usual assumptions of intuitive set theory are all true, then the set of all sets that are not members of themselves is a member of the set of all sets that are not members of themselves if and only if the set of all sets that are not members of themselves is not a member of the set of all sets that are not members of themselves. Therefore, the usual assumptions of intuitive set theory are not all true.

4. If the Administration pursues a tight-money policy, then either the leaders of the opposition party support a tight-money policy or else they denounce governmental meddling. If the leaders of the opposition party support a tight money policy and the economy goes steadily downhill, then they'll denounce governmental meddling and claim that their party could get the economy back on its feet. So if the Administration pursues a tight-money policy, then if the economy goes steadily downhill the leaders of the opposition party will denounce governmental meddling.

H. The following problems are challenging! (Wilson, p.174.)

1. (B & Q) v T
    (T ⊃ C) & (C ⊃ Q)
    ∴ Q

2. X ⊃ R
    Q ⊃ ~B
    R ⊃ B
    (~Q ⊃ ~O) & (~O ⊃ ~R)
    ∴ X

Chapter Twelve

Proofs Using UI and EG

A. The following are examples of proofs that are translated and completed:

1. All men are vain or greedy.
   Greedy men are doomed.
   Socrates is a man.
   Socrates is not doomed. /∴ Socrates is vain.

1. $(\forall x)[Mx \supset (Vx \lor Gx)]$		
2. $(\forall x) [(Mx \cdot Gx) \supset Dx]$		
3. Ms		
4. ~Ds		
5. Vs ∨ Gs	1,3 UQE	
6. ~Vs	AP	
7. Gs	5,6 DS	
8. Ms & Gs	3,7 Conj	
9. Ds	2,8 UQE	
10. Ds & ~DS	4,9 Conj	
11. Vs	6-10 IP	

2. Al and Bill are dentists.
   Every dentist golfs or plays tennis.
   Al doesn't play golf.
   Bill doesn't play tennis. /∴ Some dentists golf and some don't.

1. Da & Db	
2. $(\forall x) [Dx \supset (Gx \lor Tx)]$	
3. ~Ga	
4. ~Tb	
5. Da	1 Simp
6. Db	1 Simp
7. Gb ∨ Tb	2,6 UQE
8. Gb	4,7 DS
9. $(\exists x) (Dx \& Gx)$	6,8 EQI
10. $(\exists x) (Dx \& {\sim}Gx)$	3,5 EQI
11. $(\exists x)(Dx \& Gx) \& (\exists x) (Dx \& {\sim}Gx)$	
	9,10 Conj

B. Using the rules EQI and UQE (together with the rules of sentence logic), prove that each is valid.

1. 1. Ha & Cb
   2. $(\forall x) (Hx \supset Jx)$
   3. $(\forall x) (Cx \supset Jx)$ /∴ Ja & Jb

2. 1. Ha & Gb
   2. Ha ⊃ Ja
   3. Gb ⊃ Jb /∴ $(\exists x) (Hx \& Jx) \&\cdot (\exists x) (Gx \& Jx)$

3.1. Da & Ea
 2. Ea ⊃ (Ga ∨ Fa)
 3. ~Fa ∨ Ha
 4. Da ⊃ ~Ha /∴ (∃x: Gx)Ex

4.1. Tb & Fb
 2. (∀x: Tx)Rx
 3. (∀x: Rx & Fx)Mx /∴ (∃x: Tx)Mx

5.1. Fa & Hb
 2. (∀x: Hx)Jx
 3. (∀x: Fx)(Jx & ~Hx) /∴ (∃x: Jx)~Hx & (∃x: Jx)Hx

6.1. (∀x: Ax& Bx)Cx
 2. (∀x: Cx)(Dx ∨ Ex)
 3. ~Ea /∴ (Aa & ~Da)~Ba

7.1. Ba & Bb
 2. (∀x: Bx)Dx
 3. (Da & Ea) ⊃ Gb /∴ Ea ⊃ (∃x: Bx & Dx)Gx

C. Prove the validity of the following. (Manicus and Kruger, p.205.)

1. If Alphonse is going, everybody is; but if Alfonse doesn't go, then neither will Harry. Harrry is going, so everybody is. (Fa = Alphonse is going; Fx = x is going; Fb = Harry is going.)

2. Nobody loves Sam and Bobbie is somebody, so Bobbie doesn't love Sam. [Symbolize (x)[(X is a person ⊃ ~(x loves Sam)]; (a is a person); ∴ ~(a loves Sam).]

3. Every karate expert practices zen; Shizuo Nakamura is a karate expert; hence there are zen practicers. (Fx = x is a karate expert; Gx = x practices zen; etc.)

4. Moby Dick is a whale only if there are white whates; if there are white whales, then whales are fictitious; Moby Dick is a whale; hence he in not a whale unless he is fictitious. (Fx = x is a whale; Gx = x is white; Hx = x is fictitious, etc.)

5. There are souls , or there are minds, only if everything is spiritual. But since some things are not spiritual, it follows that there are things which are not souls and not minds. (Fx = x is a soul; Gx = x is a mind; Hx = x is spiritual.)

D. Prove the following. If necessary or convenient, use conditional proof and reduction ad absurdum. (Manicus and Kruger, pp. 205-206.)

1. Fortune tellers are never Gypsies, so if Tomara is a fortune teller, she is not a gypsy. (Fx = x is a fortune teller; Gx = x is a Gypsy, etc.)

2. Nothing is impossible; hence something is possible.

3. Either Ronald Reagan is a conservative, or everything is goofy; but there are some things which are not goofy; so Ronald Reagan is a conservative. (Fx = x is a conservative; Gx = x is goofy.)

4. Unhappy beings are either ill-fed or ill-housed; if anything is ill-fed it ought to be on welfare; Leo the lion is unhappy but well-housed; therefore Leo the lion ought to be on welfare. (Fx = x is unhappy; Gx = x is ill-fed; Hx = x is ill-housed; Jx = x ought to be on welfare.)

5. If today is Monday and the Mets are in last place, then New Yorkers are all sad. Mayor Beame is a New Yorker and today is Monday, so if the Mets are in last place, he is sad. (p = today is Monday; q = the Mets are in last place; Fx = x is a New Yorker; Gx = x is sad.)

6. Whoever dances a belly dance has good stomach muscles and is not Greek. Aphrodite belly dances, so she is not Greek. (Fx = x belly dances; Gx = x has good stomach muscles; Hx = x is Greek, etc.)

7. Everything is ultimately spiritual; hence there are things which are spiritual or there are things which are material.

8. Movie stars are affable only if affable people make good politicians; but movie stars are affable; hence, if Ronald Reagan is a movie star, he is a good politician. (Fx =x is a movie star; Gx = x is aggable; Hx =x is a good politician, etc.)

9. If there are bald German Sheperds, then the Mets will win the pennant or I will eat my hat; I will neither eat my hat nor will the Mets win the pennant; hence it is false that there are bald German Sheperds.

10. Hippies are cute and cute people are tolerable. But tolerable people are not guilty of subversion. Larry is a hippie, so how can you say that he is guilty of subversion?

Chapter Thirteen

Proofs Using EI and UG

A. In this section we shall simply offer a series of valid proofs. They should be studied so as to get acquainted with various strategies in using the rules at our disposal. (Manicus and Kruger, pp. 211-212.)

1.1.	(x)Fx	/∴ ~(∃x)~Fx
2.	(∃x)~Fx	Assume for Conditionalization
3.	~Fx	2, EI x
4.	(∃x)~Fx ⊃ ~Fx	2 and 3, Conditionalization
5.	Fx	1, UI
6.	~~Fx	5, D.N.
7.	~(∃x)~Fx	4 and 6, Modus Ponens

2.1.	(∃x)(p V Fx)	/∴ p V (∃x)Fx
2.	p V Fx	1, EI x
3.	Fx	Assume for Conditionalization
4.	(∃x)Fx	3, EG
5.	Fx ⊃ (∃x)Fx	3 and 4, Conditionalization
6.	~p ⊃ Fx	2, Imp.
7.	~p ⊃ (∃x)Fx	5 and 6, H.S.
8.	p V (∃x)Fx	7, Imp.

3.1.	(x)[Gx ⊃ (Fx v Hx)]	
2.	(∃x)(Gx & ~Hx)	/∴ (∃x)(Fx & ~Hx)
3.	Gx & ~Hx	2, EI x
4.	Gx ⊃ (Fx v Hx)	1, UI
5.	Gx	3, Simplification
6.	Fx v Hx	4 and 5, Modus Ponens
7.	~Hx & Gx	3, Commutation
8.	~Hx	7, Simplification
9.	Hx v Fx	6, Commutation
10.	Fx	8 and 9, D.S.
11.	Fx & ~Hx	8 and 10, Conjunction
12.	(∃x)(Fx & ~Hx)	11, EG

4.1. (∃x)(Fx vGx)
   2. ~(∃x)Gx   /∴(∃x)Fx
   3. ~(∃x)Fx   Assume for *Reductio Ad Absurdum*
   4. Fx v Gx   1, EI x
   5. (x)~Gx   2, Equivalence
   6. (x)~Fx   3, Equivalence
   7. ~Fx   6, UI
   8. Gx   4 and 7, D.S.
   9. ~Gx   5, UI
   10. Gx & ~Gx   8 and 9, RAA

5.1. (x)(Fx ⊃ Gx)
   2. (x)(Gx & Hx ⊃ Jx)
   3. ~(∃x)~Fx   /∴(x)(Hx ⊃ Jx)
   4. (x)Fx   3, Equivalence
   5. Fx   4, UI
   6. Fx ⊃ Gx   1, UI
   7. Gx   5 and 6, Modus Ponens
   8. (Gx & Hx) ⊃ Jx   2, UI
   9. Gx ⊃ (Hx ⊃ Jx)   8, Exp.
   10. Hx ⊃ Jx   7 and 9, Modus Ponens
   11. (x)(Hx ⊃ Jx)   10, UG

B. The following proofs are partially complete. Fill in the justifications. (Churchill, pp.340-341.)

1.1. (x)(Jx ⊃ Kx)   Premise
   2. (x)(Kx ⊃ Lx)   /∴(x)(Jx ⊃ Lx)   Premise/Conclusion
   3. Jb ⊃ Kb
   4. Kb ⊃ Lb
   5. Jb ⊃ Lb
   6. (x)(Jx ⊃ Lx)

2.1. Ha & Fa   Premise
   2. (x)[(Fx V Gx) ⊃ Wx]   /∴(∃x)(Hx & Wx)   Premise/Conclusion
   3. (Fa v Ga) ⊃ Wa
   4. Fa
   5. Fa v Ga
   6. Wa
   7. Ha
   8. Ha & Wa
   9. (∃x)(Hx & Wx)

86

3.1.   (y)(Cy ⊃ Ay)   Premise
   2.   (∃y)(Cy & Fy)   /∴(∃y)(Fy & Ay)   Premise/Conclusion
   3.   Ca & Fa
   4.   Ca
   5.   Ca ⊃ Aa
   6.   Aa
   7.   Fa & Ca
   8.   Fa
   9.   Fa & Aa
  10.   (∃y)(Fy & Ay)

4.1.   (∃w)(Fw v Gw)   Premise
   2.   ~(∃w)(Gw)   /∴(∃w)(Fw)   Premise/Conclusion
   3.   Fa v Ga
   4.   (w)~Gw
   5.   ~Ga
   6.   Fa
   7.   (∃w)(Fw)

5.1.   [(x)(Mx ⊃ ~Px) & (∃x)(Mx & Sx)]   Premise
                       /∴(∃x)(Sx & ~Px)   Conclusion
   2.   (∃x)(Mx & Sx)
   3.   Ma & Sa
   4.   (x)(Mx ⊃ ~ Px)
   5.   Ma ⊃ ~ Pa
   6.   Ma
   7.   ~ Pa
   8.   Sa
   9.   Sa & ~ Pa
  10.   (∃x)(Sx & ~Px)

6.1.   (∃x)(Fx & Gx) ⊃ (x)~(Jx ⊃Kx)   Premise
   2.   (∃x)(Jx ⊃Kx)   /∴(x)(Fx ⊃ ~Gx)   Premise/Conclusion
   3.   (∃x)(Fx & Gx) ⊃ ~(∃x)(Jx ⊃ Kx)
   4.   ~~(∃x)(Jx ⊃ Kx)
   5.   ~(∃x)(Fx & Gx)
   6.   (x)~(Fx & Gx)
   7.   (x)(~Fx V ~Gx)
   8.   (x)(Fx ⊃ ~Gx)

7.1. (z)[Gz ⊃ (Fz V Hz)]   Premise
 2. (∃z)(Gz & ~Hz)   /∴(∃z)(Fz & ~Hz)   Premise/Conclusion
 3. Ga & ~Ha
 4. Ga ⊃ (Fa V Ha)
 5. Ga
 6. Fa V Ha
 7. ~Ha
 8. Fa
 9. Fa & ~Ha
 10. (∃z)(Fz & ~Hz)

8.1. ~(x)(Fx V Gx)   Premise
 2. (y)[(Gy V Hy) ⊃ Ky   /∴(∃z)Kz   Premise/Conclusion
 3. (∃x)(Fx V Gx)
 4. ~(Fa V Ga)
 5. ~Fa & ~Ga
 6. ~Ga
 7. (~Ga V Ha) ⊃ Ka
 8. ~Ga V Ha
 9. Ka
 10. (∃z)Kz

9.1. (x)(Fx ⊃ Gx)   Premise
 2. (y)[Gy & (Hy ⊃ Jy)]   Premise
 3. ~(∃z)~Fz   /∴(w)(Hw ⊃ Jw)   Premise/Conclusion
 4. (z)~~Fz
 5. (z)Fz
 6. Fa
 7. Fa ⊃ Ga
 8. Ga
 9. Ga & (Ha ⊃ Ja)
 10. Ha ⊃ Ja
 11. (w)(Hw ⊃ Jw)

C. Each of the following is a correct deduction; the first two lines are premises. Explain the justification for each further step, and say what the deduction shows. (Barker, pp. 126-127.)

1.1. (∃x)Fx   2.1. (y)Hy
 2. (x)~Fx   2. ~(∃y)Hy
 3. Fa   3. (y)~Hy
 4. ~Fa   4. Hb
 5. Fa & ~Fa   5. ~Hb
                             6. Hb & ~Hb

88

3.1. (z)(Hz ⊃ Kz)
  2. ~(∃z)(Hz ⊃ Kz)
  3. Ha ⊃ Ka
  4. (z)~(Hz ⊃ Kz)
  5. ~(Ha ⊃ Ka)
  6. (Ha ⊃ Ka) & ~(Ha ⊃ Ka)

5.1. ~(∃x)Hx
  2. ~[~(x)Hx]
  3. (x)~Hx
  4. ~Ha
  5. (x)Hx
  6. Ha
  7. Ha & ~Ha

7.1. (z)(Hz ⊃~Fz)
  2. (∃)(Hz & Fz)
  3. Ha & Fa
  4. Ha ⊃ ~Fa
  5. Ha
  6. ~Fa
  7. Fa
  8. Fa & ~Fa

9.1. (x)(Hx ≡ Gx)
  2. (∃z)(Hz & ~Gz)
  3. Ha & ~Ga
  4. Ha ≡ Ga
  5. (Ga ⊃ Ha) & (Ha ⊃ Ga)
  6. Ha ⊃ Ga
  7. Ha
  8. Ga
  9. ~Ga
  10. Ga & ~Ga

4.1. (x)Gx
  2. ~(z)Gz
  3. (∃z)~Gz
  4. ~Gb
  5. Gb
  6. Gb & ~Gb

6.1. (y)(Hy & Gy)
  2. ~(∃y)Gy
  3. (y)~Gy
  4. Ha & Ga
  5. ~Ga
  6. Ga
  7. Ga & ~Ga

8.1. (y)(Fy ⊃Hy)
  2. (∃y)(Fy & ~Hy)
  3. Fb & ~Hb
  4. Fb ⊃ Hb
  5. Fb
  6. Hb
  7. ~Hb
  8. Hb & ~Hb

10.1. (y)(Hy ⊃ Fy) & (∃z)Hz
  2. (x)(Hx ⊃ ~Fx)
  3. (y)(Hy ⊃ Fy)
  4. (∃z)Hz
  5. Ha
  6. Ha ⊃ ~Fa
  7. Ha ⊃ Fa
  8. ~Fa
  9. Fa
  10. Fa & ~Fa

D. Prove each of the following: (Manicus and Kruger, pp. 212-213.)

1. 1. (x)(Fx ⊃Gx)
   2. (∃x)Fx   /∴(∃x)Gx

2. 1. (x)(Fx ≡ Gx)
   2. (x)(Gx ⊃ ~Ix)   /∴(x)(Fx ⊃ ~Ix)

3. **1.** (∃x)(Fx & Gx & Hx)
   2. (x)[(Fx & Gx) ⊃ ~Ix]   /∴(∃x)(Hx & ~Ix)

4. **1.** (∃x)(Fx V Hx)
   2. (x)~Fx   /∴(∃x)Gx

5. **1.** (x)(Fx ⊃ Hx)
   2. (∃x)(~Hx & ~Ix)   /∴~(x)(Fx V Ix)

6. **1.** (∃x)[(Fx & Gx) V Hx]
   2. (x)(Fx ⊃ ~Jx)
   3. ~(∃x)Hx   /∴(∃x)(Gx & ~Jx)

7. **1.** ~(∃x)(Fx & ~Gx)
   2. (x)~(Gx & Hx)
   3. (∃x)(Fx & ~Ix)   /∴(∃x)~Hx V (∃x)Ix

8. **1.** (∃x)(Fx & Gx) ⊃ (p ⊃ q)
   2. (x)(Hx) & p
   3. ~q V ~(∃x)Hx   /∴~(∃x)(Fx & Gx)

9. **1.** (x)(Fx ⊃ Hx)
   2. Ha ⊃ p
   3. Fa   /∴p

10. **1** ~(∃x)~(Fx ⊃ Gx)
   2. ~(Ga V Ha)
   3. (x)[~(Fx & Ix) ⊃ Jx]   /∴(∃x)~Jx

11. There are no sailors who get seasick on aircraft carriers, but there are sailors who get seasick on LSD's and destroyers. Hence, some sailors who get sick on destroyers do not get sick on carriers. (Fx = x is a sailor; Gx = x gets seasick on aircraft carriers; Hx = x gets sick on LSD's; Jx = x gets sick on destroyers.)

12. Ryan is Irish or he doesn't like potatoes. Irishmen invariably drink beer and eat cornbeef and cabbage on St. Patrick's Day. Ryan does like potatoes; so he drinks beer on St. Patrick's Day. (Fx = x is Irish; Gx = x likes potatoes; Hx = x drinks beer; Jx = x eats cornbeef and cabbage on St. Patrick's Day.)

13. A male cannot enter the girls' dormitory unless a proctor is available. Last Tuesday, some male students were in the dorm. Hence a proctor must have been available. (Fx = x is a male; Gx = x enters the girls' dormitory; p = a proctor is available; Hx = x is a student.)

14. Cigarette smokers may end up with cancer and alcoholics may ruin their livers and get *delirium tremens*. So, if you are both a cigarette smoker and an alcoholic, you may end up with cancer, a ruined liver, or *delirium tremens*. (Fx = x smokes cigarettes; Gx = x may end up with cancer; Hx = x is an alcoholic; Jx = x may ruin his liver; Kx = x may get *delirium tremens*.)

E. Prove that each of the following is valid. (McKay, pp. 231-232)

    1. (∃x) (Fx & Gx)
       (x) (Gx ⊃ Hx)
       ∴ (∃x) (Fx & Hx)

    2. (∃x) (Fx & Gx)
       ∴ (∃x) (Gx & Fx)

    3. (∃x) (Fx & Gx)
       (∃x) (Fx & Hx)
       (x) (Hx ⊃ Kx)
       (x) (Gx & ~Kx)
       ∴ (∃x) (Fx & Kx) & (∃x) (Fx & ~Kx)

    4. (∃x) (Fx & Gx) (Fa & Ja)
       (∃x) (Fx & Ex)
       (x) [Ex ⊃ (Gx & Hx)]
       (x) (Jx ⊃ Kx)
       ∴ (∃x) (Fx & Kx)

    5. Ba & (∃x) (Bx & ~Fx)
       (x) (Bx ⊃ Ax)
       (Aa & Ca) ⊃ (x) [(Bx & ~Fx) ⊃ Gx]
       ∴ Ca ⊃ (∃x)[(Gx & ~Fx) & Ax]

    6. (∃x)(Fx & Gx)
       (x) (Fx ⊃ Hx)
       ∴ (∃x) (Hx & Gx)

F. Translate the following and, if valid, prove. (Manicas and Kruger, p.214.)

    1. Professors may be either just or merciful, and sympathetic professors are not just. Hence if anyone is a professor, then if he is sympathetic, he is merciful. (Fx = x is a professor; Gx = x is just; Hx = x is merciful; Jx = x is sympathetic.)

2. Either gambling is immoral or it is unnecessary. A lottery is a form of gambling. But since nothing which promotes good is immoral and some lotteries do promote good, there are lotteries which are unnecessary. (Fx = x is gambling; Gx = x is moral; Hx = x is necessary; Jx = x is a lottery; Kx = x promotes good.)

3. A person is authoritarian if and only if he is militant. Tyrants are all Janus-faced. Each and every militant is neurotic, and if anyone is Janus-faced, then he is successful. Since there are authoritarians who are tyrants, there are successful neurotics. (Fx = x is authoritarian; Gx = x is militant; Hx = x is a tyrant; Jx = x is Janus-faced; Kx = x is neurotic; Lx = x is successful.)

4. If God exists, then something is neither false nor evil. Everything which is either true or good is beautiful. There is a God who is merciful and just. Hence there is beauty. (Fx = x is a God; Gx = x is false; Hx = x is evil; Jx = x is beautiful; Kx = x is merciful; Lx = x is just.)

5. Something is beautiful only if love is beautiful; something is tragic only if all beautiful things are tragic. Something is both beautiful and tragic; hence love is tragic. (Fx = x is beautiful; Gx = x is love; Hx = x is tragic.)

6. Mini-boppers who major in philosophy are Fulbright Fellows, and only students with good grades are Fulbright Fellows. Still, if there are students with good grades who are not gorgeous, then no students with good grades are boys. So, there are some Fulbright Fellows who are not gorgeous only if there are no mini-boppers who are boys and philosophy majors. (Fx = x is a mini-bopper; Gx = x majors in philosophy; Hx = x is a Fulbright Fellow; Jx = x is a student with good grades; Kx = x is gorgeous; Lx = x is a boy.)

G. Translate the following. If valid, prove. (Klein)

1. If philosophy is really worthwhile, then everyone should take at least on course. But philosophy is only worthwhile if one is both committed and clever. There exists at least one person who is committed and clever , therefore philosophy must be worthwhile.

2. Feminism is a philosophical position. However, all philosophical positions must maintain a commitment, at some level, to the law of non-contradiction. Any position that is meaningful maintains a commitment to the law of non-contradiction. So Feminism is not meaningful.

3. Postmodern philosophy is fundamentally different from Deconstruction. All postmodern philosophy maintains some commitment to Plato. All commitments to Plato are commitments accepted by Deconstruction. Therefore, if anything counts as Deconstruction it cannot count as Postmodern.

4. Anyone in business is said to only care about the "bottom line". But there are serious philosophers in business who claim to care about something more. Whatever one claims to care about they must really think is true. So it must be true that philosophers only care about the "bottom line"

92

5. It is said that tenure is a necessary part of any academic institution. But tenure does not necessarily protect anyone who is a good teacher and fine scholar. Of course protecting good teachers and fine scholars is the point of any academic institution. Therefore, it is not the case that tenure is a necessary part of an academic institution.

Chapter Fourteen

More Difficult Proofs Using All Quantification Rules

A. Using all four quantification rules when necessary, deduce the conclusions of the following arguments from their premise. (Gustason, p. 210.)

1.1. (x)(Ax ⊃ Bx)
   2. (x)(Bx ⊃ Cx) /∴ (x)(Ax ⊃ Cx)

2.1. (x)(Dx ⊃ Ex)
   2. (y)(Ey ⊃ Fy) /∴(z)(Dz ⊃ Fz)

3.1. (x)[Ax ⊃ (Bx & Cx)]
   2. ~Bx /∴~Ad

4.1. (x)[Dx ⊃ (Ex & Fx)]
   2. (∃x)~Fx /∴(∃x)~Dx

5.1. (x)(Mx ⊃ ~Lx)
   2. (∃x)(Nx & Lx) /∴(∃x)(Nx & ~Mx)

6.1. (x)[(Bx v Cx) ⊃ Dx]
   2. (∃y)(~Cy v ~By)
   3. (∃z)[~(Ez v ~Cz)] /∴(∃x)Dx

7.1. (∃x)[Ax & (y)(By ⊃ Rxy)]
   2. (x)[Ax ⊃ (y)(Sy ⊃ ~Rxy)] /∴(x)(Bx ⊃ ~Sx)

8. All gods are immortal. All gods are moral. Zeus is immoral and Socrates is mortal. Therefore, neither Socrates nor Zeus is a god. (Gx = x is a god; Mx = x is mortal; Rx = x is moral; d = Zeus; s = Socrates.)

9. All multiples of six are multiples of two and also multiples of three. All multiples of two are even. Therefore, all multiples of six are even. (Mxy = x is a multiple of y; f = six; b = two; c = three; Ex = x is even.)

10. All even numbers are multiples of either six or two. All multiples of six are multiples of two. Therefore, all even numbers are multiples of two. (Same notation as above.)

11. Every triangle is either scalene or isosceles. Isosceles and equilateral triangles are symmetrical. Therefore, all triangles that are not scalene are symmetrical. (Tx = x is a triangle; Sx = x is scalene; Ix = x is isosceles; Ex = x is equilateral; Rx = x is symmetrical.)

12. All moths are Lepidoptera. All insects are arthropods. So, if all Lepidoptera are insects, then all moths are arthropods. (Mx = x is a moth; Lx = x is a Lepidoptera; Ix = x is an insect; Ax = x is an arthropod.)

13. There is at least one being than whom none is greater. Therefore, for each being there exists at least one being than which it is not greater. (Gxy = x is greater than y.)

B. Prove that each is valid. (McKay, p.241.)

1.1. (x) (Fx ⊃ Gx)
  2. (x) (Hx ⊃ ~Gx) / ∴ (x) (Hx ⊃ ~Fx)

2.1. (∃x) (Hx & Fx) ⊃ (x) (Hx ⊃ Gx)/ ∴ (x) [(Hx & ~Gx) ⊃ ~Fx]

C. Using all four quantification rules when necessary deduce the conclusions of the following arguments from their premises. Check for validity if necessary. (McKay, p.202.)

1.1 (∃x)(Fx & Gx) / ∴ (∃y)Fy

2.1. (∃x)(∃y)Rxy / ∴ (∃y)(∃x)Ryx

3.1. (∃x)(Fx & Gx)
  2. (∃x)(Fx & Hx)
  3. (∃y)(Gy & Fy) ⊃ (∃x)(Gx & Hx) / ∴ (∃y)(Gy & Hy)

4.1. (∃x)Lxx / ∴ (∃x)(∃y)Lxy

5.1. (∃x)Bx ⊃ Be / ∴ (∃x)Bx ≡ Be

6.1. (∃x)[Sx & ~(Sx & Tx)] / ∴ (∃x)Sx & (∃y)~Ty

7.1. (x)(Fx ⊃ Gx) ⊃ [~(∃y)Gy ⊃ ~(∃x)Fz]
  2. (∃z)Fz / ∴ (x)(Fx ⊃ Gx) ⊃ (∃y)(Gy v Hy)

8.1. ~(∃x)(Px & ~Wx)
  2. Pa / ∴ Wa

9.1. ~(∃x)~Ix
  2. ~(∃x)~Wx / ∴ ~(∃x)(~Ix v ~Wx)

D. Construct a formal proof of validity for each of the following arguments. (Halverson, p.243.):

    1.1. (x)[Kx ⊃ (Lx & Mx)]
      2. (∃x)(Nx & ~Lx) / ∴ (∃x)(Nx & ~Kx)

    2.1. (x)[Px ⊃ (Qx & Rx)]
      2. (∃x)[Tx & ~(Qx v Rx)] / ∴ (∃x)(tx & ~Px)

    3.1. (x)(Lx ⊃ Mx)
      2. (x)[Mx ⊃ ~(Qx & Tx)] / ∴ (x)[Qx ⊃ (~Tx v ~Lx)]

    4.1. (x)[Jx ⊃ (Ax ≡ Rx)]
      2. (∃x)(Jx & ~Ax) / ∴ (∃x)(Jx & ~Rx)

    5.1. (∃x)(Ax & Sx)
      2. (x)[Sx ⊃ (Tx v Rx)] / ∴ (∃x)[Ax & (~Tx ⊃ Rx)]

    6.1. (x)[Ax ⊃ (Bx v Cx)]
      2. (x)(Cx ⊃ Dx)
      3. (x)~Dx / ∴ (x)(Ax ⊃ Bx)

    7.1. (x)(Hx ⊃ Sx)
      2. (x)(Sx ⊃ Qx)
      3. (∃x)(Ex & ~Qx) / ∴ (∃x)(Ex & ~Hx)

    8.1. (x)(Jx ⊃ Kx)
      2. (x)(Rx ⊃ ~Kx)
      3. (∃x)(Tx & Rx) / ∴ (∃x)(Tx & ~Jx)

E. Construct a formal proof for each of the arguments below. Check for validity if necessary. (Halverson, p. 244.)

    1. All Pontiacs are comfortable-riding automobiles, but none of the cars in the motor pool are comfortable to ride in, so it is obvious that none of the cars in the pool are Pontiacs. (Px = x is a Pontiac; Cx = x is a comfortable to ride in; Mx = x is in the motor pool.)

    2. None of the pilots on this list are over fifty years of age. To qualify as a senior citizen, however, one must be at least sixty-five years old, so it is clear that none of these pilots are senior citizens. (Px = x is a pilot; Ox = x is at least sixty-five years old; Sx = x is a senior citizen.)

3. All of the members of this class are either freshman or juniors. The students in North Dorm, however, are all seniors. Obviously, if one is a senior one is neither a freshman nor a junior. Thus, none of the students in this class live in North Dorm. (Mx = x is a member of this class; Rx = x is a freshman; Jx = x is a junior; Sx = x is a senior; Nx = x lives in North Dorm.)

4. All citizens are both voters and taxpayers. None of the people in this group are voters, however, so it is clear that they are not citizens. (Cx = x is a citizen; Vx = x is a voter; Tx = x is a taxpayer; Gx = x is a person in this group.)

5. All philanthropists are both wealthy and generous. Misers, however, are not generous, so misers never become philanthropists. (Px = x is a philanthropist; Wx = x is wealthy; Gx = x is generous; Mx = x is a miser.)

6. Nobody can be simultaneously both old and young, or both rich and poor. All of the members of my club, however, are old and poor. Thus, none of them is either young or rich. (Nx = x is a person; Ox = x is old; Yx = x is young; Rx = x is rich; Px = x is poor; Cx = x is a member of my club.)

F. Construct a formal proof of validity for each of the following valid arguments. Any of our quantifier inferences may be required and may be used. (Wilson, p.272.)

1.1. $(x)(Rx \supset Tx)$
 2. $(\exists x)Rx$ /∴ $(\exists x)Tx$

2.1. $(x)[(Rx \lor Tx) \supset Qx]$
 2. $(\exists x)Rx$ /∴ $(\exists x)Qx$

3.1. $(x)(\sim Mx \supset Mx)$ /∴ $(x)Mx$

4.1. $(\exists x)Cx$
 2. $(x)[Cx \supset (Tx \& Vx)]$ /∴ $(\exists x)Tx$

5.1. $(x)(Ax \supset Ux)$
 2. $\sim Uj$ /∴ $(\exists x)\sim Ax$

6.1. $(x)(Rx \supset Tx)$
 2. $(x)(Rx \supset \sim Tx)$ /∴ $(x)\sim Rx$

7.1. $(x)(Vx \equiv Nx)$
 2. Nj /∴ $(\exists x)Vx$

8.1. $(x)(Ax \supset Bx)$ /∴ $(x)[(Ax \& Cx) \supset Bx]$

9.1. $(x)[Ax \supset (Bx \& Cx)]$ /∴ $(x)(Ax \supset Bx)$

10. 1. (x)[(Ex & Cx) ⊃ Ox]
    2. (x)(Ex ⊃ Cx) /∴(x)(Ex ⊃ Ox)

11. 1. (∃x)(Fx & Dx) /∴(∃x)Fx

12. 1. (x)[(Bx v Cx) ⊃ Kx]
    2. (x)[(Kx & Ox) ⊃ (Dx & Nx)] /∴(x)[Bx ⊃ (Ox ⊃ Nx)]

13. 1. (x)[(Ax v Bx) ⊃ (Dx & Cx)]
    2. (∃x)(Bx & Rx) /∴(∃x)(Dx & Rx)

14. 1. (x)[(Ax & Bx) ⊃Cx]
    2. (∃x)(Ax & ~Cx) /∴(∃x)~Bx

15. 1. (x)(~Hx ≡ ~Ix)
    2. (x)[(~Ix & ~Hx) ⊃ Kx]
    3. (∃x)~Ix
    4. (x)(~Ix ≡ Qx)
    5. (x)(Qx ⊃Rx) /∴(∃x)(Kx & Rx)

G. Construct a proof of validity for each of the following arguments. (Wilson, p.286.)

1. 1 Mj
   2. ~Ms /∴(∃x)Mx & (∃x)~Mx

2. 1. (∃x)(Mx & Gx) /∴(∃x)Mx & (∃x) Gx

3. 1. (x)(Ax ⊃ Hx)
   2. Rb
   3. (∃x)Ax /∴(∃x)Hx & (∃x)Rx

4. 1. (x)(Mx ⊃ Gx) /∴(x)Mx ⊃ (x)Gx

5. 1. (x)(Qx ⊃ Tx)
   2. (x)(Qx ⊃ Vx) /∴(∃x)Qx ⊃ (∃x)(Tx & Vx)

6. 1. (∃x)(Ix & Sx)
   2. (∃x)(Cx & Tx) /∴(∃x)Ix & (∃x)Cx

7. 1. (∃x)Ix ⊃ (∃x)Lx
   2. (x)(Lx ⊃ Rx)
   3. (∃x)Ix /∴(∃x)(Lx & Rx)

8.1. $(x)(Ax \equiv Bx) / \therefore (x)(Ax \supset Bx) \& (x)(Bx \supset Ax)$

9.1. $(x)(Ax \supset Bx) \& (x)(Bx \supset Ax) / \therefore (x)(Ax \equiv Bx)$

10.1 $(x)[(Rx \& Sx) \supset Tx]$
   2. $(\exists x)Rx / \therefore (x)Sx \supset (\exists x)Tx$

H. Demonstrate the validity of each of the following arguments. (Churchill, pp. 341-342.)

1. All Zionists are Jewish, and no Moslems are Jewish. However, there are Moslems who are Israelites. Thus, some Israelites are not Zionists. ($Zx = x$ is a Zionist; $Jx = x$ is Jewish; $Mx = x$ is Moslem; $Ix = x$ is an Israeli.)

2. All screen stars are attractive. Some screen stars are feminists. All attractive persons are envied persons. Thus, some feminists are envied persons. ($Sz = z$ is a screen star; $Az = z$ is attractive; $Fz = z$ is a feminist; $Ez = z$ is envied.)

3. Every Basque is either Spanish or French. There are non-Spanish Basques. Therefore, some Basques are French. ($Bx = x$ is a Basque; $Sx = x$ is Spanish; $Fx = x$ Is French.)

4. Any act of violence is either dangerous or foolhardy. Anything that is either dangerous or foolhardy is immoral. Thus, if anything is desirable, then if it is violent, then it is immoral. ($Vy = y$ is violent; $Dy = y$ is dangerous; $Fy = y$ is foolhardy; $Iy = y$ is immoral; $Sy = y$ is desirable.)

5. If Alex passes, then everybody will; but if Alex doesn't pass, then neither will Brett. Brett will pass, so everybody will. ($Px = x$ will pass; $a = $ Alex; $b = $ Brett.)

6. "All babies are illogical. No one is despised who can manage a crocodile. Illogical persons are despised. Therefore, no baby can manage a crocodile." –Lewis Carroll, *Symbolic Logic* ($Bx = x$ is a baby; $Ix = x$ is illogical; $Mx = x$ can manage a crocodile; $Dx = x$ is despised.)

7. Not all of the rebels were unsuccessful. None but the unsuccessful were martyrs. The only rebels were new converts. Consequently, at least some of the new converts weren't martyred. ($Rz = z$ is a rebel; $Sz = z$ is successful; $Mz = z$ Is a martyr; $Cz = z$ is a new convert.)

8. There are souls or there are minds only if everything is spiritual. But since some things are not spiritual, it follows that there are things that are not souls and not minds. ($Sx = x$ is a soul; $Mx = x$ is a mind; $Px = x$ is spiritual.)

9. Standard IQ tests are culturally biased. Anything that is culturally biased is discriminatory. But whatever is constitutional to use in public schools is nondiscriminatory. So, standard IQ tests are not constitutional to use in public schools. (Sw = w is a standard IQ test; Cw = w is culturally biased; Dw = w is discriminatory; Uw = w is constitutional to use in public schools.)

10. If an only if a woman's potentialities are fulfilled is her life a success. Hence, if either her potentialities are fulfilled or her life is a success, then both her potentialities are fulfilled and her life is a success. (Domain = Women; Px = x has fulfilled potentiality; Sx = x has a successful life.) *Hint*: (p ≡ q) is equivalent to (p & q) or (~p & ~q).

I. Prove validity by constructing a formal proof, or prove invalidity by using the partial-truth-table method.

1. If some drugs have adverse reactions, then no drugs should be prescribed without careful supervision. Some monoamine oxidase inhibitors have caused death. Any drug that has caused death has adverse reactions! Hence, no drugs should be prescribed without careful supervision. (Domain = drugs; Ax = x has adverse reactions; Px = x should be prescribed; Cx = x is carefully supervised; Mx = x is a monoamine oxidase inhibitor; Dx = x has caused death.)

2. Icarus had artificial wings that were held together with wax. If anyone flies near the sun with artificial wings that are held together with wax, then someone will fall to the earth. Icarus flew near the sun. Hence, someone will fall to the earth. (Ax = x has artificial wings that are held together with wax; Fx = x flies near the sun; Ex = x falls to the earth.)

3. Whenever someone steals, then everyone pays higher prices. Smitty hasn't had to pay higher prices. Hence, no one has stolen. (Sx = x steals; Px = x pays higher prices; s = Smitty.)

4. "All our yesterdays have lighted fools the way to dusty death" (Shakespeare, *Macbeth*). If all of us have yesterdays, then all of us have yesterdays that have lighted fools the way to dusty death. (Yx = x is a person's yesterday; Lx = x has lighted fools the way to dusty death.)

5. If what's good for General Motors is good for the country*, then whatever eliminates foreign competition is good for the country. Tough trade laws eliminate foreign competition. Hence, tough trade laws are good for the country. (Gx = x is good for General Motors; Cx = x is good for the country; Ex = x eliminates foreign competition; Lx = x is a tough trade law.) (*This statement was made by Charles E. Wilson when he was president of General Motors Corporation.)

J. Offer your own intuitions about the metalogical justifications for the different Quantification Rules—UI, EG EI and UG. Discuss their similarities, differences and the need for the various restrictions on EI and UG.

Chapter Fifteen

Proofs Using Relations

A. Prove the following. (McKay, p. 243)

1. (x)(Fx ⊃ Hxa)
    (∃x)(Gx & Hax)
    [(x) (Fx V Gx) ⊃ (y)Hxy] ⊃ [(z)(Hzy ⊃ Hxz)]
    Fb & [(y)Fy ⊃(z)(Gz ⊃ Hyz)]
    ∴ [Hba & (∃x)(Gx & Hbx)] & [(∃y)Gy &(∃z)(Gz & Hyz)]

2. (x)[(∃y)(Ay & Rxy) ⊃ Rxa]
    (∃x)(Ax & Rax)
    ~(x)(Cx ⊃ Bx)
    (x)(Rxa ⊃ Bx)
    ∴[(x)(Ax & Rxx) ⊃ Bx] & [(∃x)Rxx & (∃y)(Ay & Rxy)] &[(∃x)Cx&(y)(Ay⊃~Rxy)]

3. (∃x)(Fx & Rxx)
    (x)[(∃y)(Fy & Ryx) ⊃Gx]
    (∃x)(Hx & Rxx)
    ∴ [~(x)(Fx ⊃ Hx) & (∃y)(Fy & Gy)] & [(z)(~Gz) ⊃ ~(∃y)(Fy & Ryz)]

4. ~(∃x)(Ax) & [(∃y)(By & Rxy) & Rxb]
    (x)(Rxx ⊃ Rxb)
    ∴ (x)[(Ax & Rxx) ⊃ ~Bx]

5. (x)[(∃y)(Fy & Rxy) ⊃ Hx]
    Fa
    (∃x)(Fx & Hx) ⊃ (x)(Hx ⊃ Gx)
    (∃x)(Hx & ~Gx)
    ∴ ~(x)[Fx ⊃ (∃y)(Fy & Rxy)]

6. (x)[Fx ⊃ (y)(Fy & Rxy) ⊃ Ryx]
    Rab & (Fa & Fb)
    (x)[(∃y)(Fy & Rxy) ⊃ Rxx]
    (∃x)[Fx & ~(∃y)(Fy & Rxy)]
    ∴ [Rbb & (∃x)(Fx & ~Rxb)] & (x)[(Fx & Rbx) ⊃ Rxx]

7. (x)[Ax ⊃ (∃y)(By & Rxy)]
   (x)(Bx ⊃ Ax)
   ~(∃x)[Ax & (~Bx V ~Cx)]
   ∴(x)[Ax ⊃ (∃y)(Ay &Rxy)] & (x)[Ax ⊃ (∃y)(Cy & Rxy)]

8. (x){Fx ⊃ (y)[(Fy & Gy) ⊃ Rxy]}
   (∃y)[Gy & (x)(Fx ⊃ ~Rxy)]
   ∴ (∃x)(Gx & ~Fx) & ((∃x)(Gx & Fx) ⊃ {(x)[Fx ⊃[(∃y)(Gy & Rxy) & (∃z)(Gz & ~Rxz)]})

9. (x)(Fx ⊃ Rxa)
   (∃x)(Gx & Rax)
   (x)(Fx VGx) ⊃ (y)[Rxy ⊃ (z)(Ryz ⊃ Rxz)]
   Fb & (y)[Fy ⊃ (∃z)(Gz & Rzy)]
   ∴ Rba &{(∃x)(Gx & Rbx) & (∃y)[Gy & (∃z)(Gz & Ryz)]}

10. (x)[(∃y)(Ay & Rxy) ⊃ Rxa]
   (∃x)(Gx & Rax)
   ~(x)(Cx ⌣ Bx)
   (x)(Rxa ⊃ Bx)
   ∴(x){[(Ax & Rxx) ⊃ Bx] & (∃x)[Rxx & (∃y)(Ay & Ryy)] & (∃x)[Cx & (y)(Ay ⊃ ~Rxy)]}

B. Deduce the conclusion of each of the following arguments from its premises; be prepared to combine and modify strategies already used, and to invent some new ones of your own. (McKay, p.222.)

1. (∃x) (Px & Lxa)
   (y) (Py ⊃ Lay)
   (x)(y) [(Lxa & Lay) ⊃ Lxy]
   ∴ (∃x) [Px & (y)(Py ⊃ Lay)]

2. (x)(y) (Sxy ⊃ Syx)
   (x) (Sxd ⊃ ~Tbx)
   (x)(y) (Rax ⊃ Txy)
   ∴ Rab ⊃ ~sdc

3. (∃x)(Fx) ⊃ (y) (Ay ⊃ By)
   (∃x)(Gx) ⊃ (y) (Cy ⊃ ~By)
   ∴ (∃x) (Gx & Fx) ⊃ (y) (Cy ⊃ ~Ay)

4. (x) (Cx ⊃ Fx)
   ∴ (x) [(∃y) (Cy & Dxy) (∃z) (Fz & Dxz)]

5. (x) (∃y) (Lxy)
   ∴ (y) (∃z) (Lyz)

C. Some of the following arguments are valid and some are invalid. Symbolize each. Then deduce the conclusions of the valid ones from their premises. (McKay, pp.222-224.)

1. Everyone doubts something or other. Anyone who doubts something can be certain of at least one thing. Therefore each person can be certain of at least one thing. (Px = x is a person; Dxy = x doubts y; Cxy = x can be certain of y.)

2. Some sentences have truth-values. No pattern of marks traced in the sand by the wind has a truth-value. Therefore, some patterns of marks traced in the sand by the wind are not sentences. (Sx = x is a sentence; Tx = x has a truth-value; Px x= is a pattern of marks traced in the sand by the wind.)

3. If there is a bull market underway, then only glamor stocks rise faster than International Toothpick. A competitor of International Toothpick is rising faster than it. Therefore, if none of International Totthpick's competitors are glamor stocks, no bull market is underway. (Bx = x is a bull market; Ux = x is underway; Gx = x is a glamor stock; Rxy = x is rising faster than y; i = International Toothpick; Cxy = x is a competitor of y.)

4. If one thing resembles a second thing, then the second resembles the first. If one thing resembles a second thing and the second resembles a third, then the first thing resembles the third. Therefore everything resembles itself. (Rxy = x resembles y.)

5. Every valid argument Jones presented today was unsound. An argument is sound if and only if it is valid and all its premises are true. Therefore if the Ontological Argument is one of the valid arguments Jones presented today, at least one of its premises is untrue. (Vx = x is valid; Ax = x is an argument; j = Jones; Pxy = x presented y today; Sx = x is sound; Rxy = x is a premise of y; Tx = x is true; a = the Ontological Argument.)

6. Every spy who was undetected eluded at least one guard. Some spies were armed and so was each guard they eluded. No armed spy was detected. Therefore, there exists a guard who is such that he is a spy only if he was undetected. (Sx = x is a spy; Dx = x was detected; Exy = x eluded y; Gx = x is a guard; Ax = x was armed.)

7. There is a politician who is despised by all citizens who despise any politician at all. Every citizen despises at least one politician. Therefore there is a politician who is despised by every citizen. (Px = x is a politician; Dxy = x despises y; Cx = x is a citizen.)

8. For each positive integer x, there exists a sentence containing more than x words. Any sentence that contains, for each positive integer x, more than x words is of infinite length. Therefore there exists at least one sentence of infinite length. (Ix = x is a positive integer; Sx = x is a sentence; Cxy = x contains more than y words; Lx = x is of infinite length.)

104

9. If each positive integer is such that it satisfies Goldbach's hypothesis and all smaller even integers satisfy that hypothesis, then every even integer satisfies Goldbach's hypothesis. Therefore, if for each even integer that does not satisfy Goldbach's hypothesis there exists a smaller even integer that does not satisfy it either, then all even integers satisfy Goldbach's hypothesis. (Ex = x is an even integer; Sx = x satisfies Goldbach's hypothesis; Lxy = x is less than y.)

10. If for each even integer that does not satisfy Goldbach's hypothesis there exists a smaller even integer that does not satisfy it either, then every even integer satisfies Goldbach's hypothesis. Therefore if each even integer is such that it satisfies Goldbach's hypothesis, then every even integer satisfies Goldbach's hypothesis. (Same notation as number 9.)

11. If I am morally permitted to perform any action, then everyone is morally permitted to perform that action. If something awful occurs if everyone performs a certain action then no one is morally permitted to perform that action. So if something awful occurs if I perform a certain action then I am not morally permitted to perform that action. (Mxy = x is morally permitted to perform y; Ax = x is an action; Hx = x is a person; Wx = x is awful; Ox = x occurs; Pxy = x performs y; i = me.)

12. Any argument of interest to all philosophers is worthy of everyone's attention. Anything worthy of anyone's attention ought to be considered by him. Therefore if each philosopher is interested in all arguments propounded by those who disagree with him, then any argument propounded by anyone who disagrees with all philosophers ought to be considered by everyone. (Ax = x is an argument; Ixy = x is interested in y; Px = x is a philosopher; Wxy = x is worthy of y's attention; Hx = x is a person; Oxy = x ought to consider y; Rxy = X propounds y; Dxy = x disagrees with y.)

D. Prove that each is valid. (McKay, p.227.)

8.1. Rab
2. Pa & Pb
3. (∃x: Px)Rxb ⊃ (∀x: Px)Rxb /∴ Rbb

9.1. (∀x: Fx)Gx
2. (∀x: ~Fx)(∀y: Gy)Rxy
3. (∀x: Hx)~Gx
4. Ha & Fb /∴ (∃x: ~Hx)Rax

10.1.Rab
2. (∀x:Rxb)Fx
3. ~Fb /∴ (∃x: Fx)(∃y: ~Fy)Rxy

11.1.(∀x: Ax)Bx
2. Ad & Cd /∴ (∀x: Cx)Dx ⊃ (∃x:Bx)Dx

12.1. $(\forall x: Fx)(\forall y: Gy)Rxy$
   2. Fa & (Gb & Gc)
   3. ~Rbc /∴ $(\exists x: \sim Fx)(\exists y: Jy)Ryx$

13.1. (Aa & Ca) ⊃ $(\forall x: Bx \& \sim Fx)Gx$
   2. $(\forall x: Bx)Ax$
   3. Ba & (Bb & ~Fb) /∴ Ca ⊃ $(\exists x: Gx \cdot \sim Fx)Ax$

14.1. Hb
   2. $(\forall x: Fx)Gx$
   3. (Ga · Hb) ⊃ Rab
   4. $(\forall x: Hx)Jx$ /∴ Fa ⊃ $(\exists x: Fx)(\exists y: Jy)Rxy$

15.1. (Fa & Gb) & Rab
   2. $(\forall x: Fx)Hx$
   3. $(\forall x: Gx)Kx$ /∴ $(\exists x: Hx)(\exists y: Ky)Rxy$

16.1. Fa & Ga
   2. $(\forall x: Gx)(Hx \lor \sim Fx)$
   3. $(\forall x: Fx \& Hx)(\exists y: Gy)Rxy$ /∴ $(\exists x: Gx)(\exists y: Gy)Rxy$

E. Provide a formal proof for each of the following valid arguments. (Wilson, pp. 328-329)

1. <u>Hab</u>
    ∴ $(\exists x)(\exists y)Hxy$

2. Hab
    <u>$(\exists x)(Hxb \supset Hbb)$</u>
    ∴ Hbb

3. Aab
    <u>$(\exists x)Axb \supset (x)Axb$</u>
    ∴ Abb

4. $(\exists x)Axa$
    $(x)(Axa \supset Bx)$
    <u>~Ba</u>
    ∴ $(\exists x)Bx \& (\exists x)\sim Bx$

5. <u>$(\exists x)(x)Axy$</u>
    ∴ $(x)(\exists y)Ayx$

6. <u>$(x)(Axa \supset \sim Aax)$</u>
    ∴ ~Aaa

7. $(x)(y)(Axy \supset Axa)$
    <u>$(x)(Bx\ Axb)$</u>   .
    ∴ $(x)(Bx \supset Axa)$

8. $(x)[(\exists y)(Axy) \supset (y)(Ayx)]$
    <u>$(\exists x)(\exists y)(Axy)$</u>   .
    ∴ $(\exists y)(x)(Axy)$

9. $(x)(y)[(Ax \& Bxy) \supset Cy]$
    <u>Aa</u>
    ∴ $(x)\ (Bxa \supset Cx)$

10. <u>$(x)(Rax \supset Qcxa)$</u>   .
    ∴ $(x)(Rax \supset (\exists y)(\exists z)Qyxz$

106

F. Symbolize, and provide a formal proof for each of the following valid arguments. (Wilson, p. 329.)

1. The bigger they are, the harder they fall. Nixon was bigger than most. Hence, he fell harder than most. (RD: persons; Bxy = x is bigger than y; Hxy = x falls harder than y.)

2. Everyone in Mudville is unhappy. No one who has read *The Power of Positive Thinking* is unhappy. Hence, no one in Mudville has read *The Power of Positive Thinking*. (Px = x is a person; Ixy = x is in y; Ux = x is unhappy; Rxy = x has read y.)

3. Don Juan pursued every woman he knew. There were women that Don Juan knew. Hence, there were women that Don Juan pursued. (Pxy = x pursues y; Kxy = x knows y; Wx = x is a woman.)

4. A "Don Juan" pursues every woman he knows. Don Juan was a "Don Juan" who knew (the woman) Lady Elvire. Hence, Don Juan pursued Lady Elvire. (Dx = x is a "Don Juan"; Pxy = x pursues y; Wx = x is a woman; Kxy = x knows y.)

5. If anyone finds anything, then they've looked for it. Hence, if anyone finds El Dorado, then they've looked for it. (Px = x is a person; Fxy = x finds y; Lxy = x has looked for y.)

G. Prove the following. (McKay, p.232.)

1. Fa & Ga
(x) [Gx ⊃ (Hx v ~Fx)]
(x) [(Fx & Hx) ⊃ (∃x) (Ky & Rxy)]
(x) (Kx ⊃ Jx)
∴ (∃x)[Gx & (∃x) Ky & Rxy)]

2. (∃x) [Fx & (∃x) (Gy & Rxy)]
(x) (Fx ⊃ Hx)
(x) (Gx & Kx)
∴ (∃x)[Hx & (∃x)(Ky & Rxy)]

3. (∃x) [Fx & (∃x) (Fy & Rxy)]
(x) [Fx & [(∃x) ⊃ (Gy & Rxy)] ⊃ Hx}
(x) {Fx & [(∃x) (Gy & Rxy)] ⊃ ~Hx}
(x) (Fx ⊃ Gx)
∴ (∃x)[Hx & (∃x) (~Hy & Ryx)]

4. (∃x) {[Fx & (∃x) (Gy & Ray)] & Rxa}
Ha
(x) [(∃x) (Hy & Rxy) ⊃ Hx]
(x) [(x) (Rxy ⊃Ryx)]
∴ (∃x) [Gx & (∃x) (Fy & Rxy)]

5. (x) {Fx ⊃ (y) [(Gy & Rxy) ~Ryx]}
   (∃x) (Fx & Rxx)
   ∴ (∃x) (Fx & ~Gx)

Chapter Sixteen

Flow-Charting
(Barker, pp.104-109.)

A. Logic and Computers.

1. Nowadays digital computers are rapidly altering many aspects of our lives. They have developed enormous power to perform elaborate calculations quickly, to store and sort vast amounts of information, and to control intricate machinery. Many tasks that we formerly did by hand are now being performed far more efficiently by computers, and many tasks that formerly could not be done at all are being accomplished through use of these machines.

Logic is related to computers in various ways. Some of these have to do with computer programming (the planning out of the series of steps by means of which computers are to perform specific tasks). A knowledge of logical distinctions can sometimes be most helpful, enabling the computer programmer who is acquainted with logic to avoid mistakes and find short cuts. However, we shall consider a more fundamental connection between logic and computers, having to do with the basic electric structure of the digital computer, which is strongly analogous to the logic of truth functions.

A digital computer is built up of various types of basic units, each of which can be regarded as a kind of switching circuit. By a switching circuit we mean a device having one or more "input" terminals and one or more "output" terminals. The device is built in such a way that the voltage at the output terminals is related to the voltage at the input terminals according to some regular, definite pattern so that the input voltages determine the output voltages. (When we speak of "input" and "output" here we do not mean that any palpable thing is put in or taken out; it is just that the voltage at the so-called input terminals will correspond to some initial information, while the voltage at the output terminals will correspond to some other information calculated from the initial information.)

The computer as a whole is a network of these basic units wired together. The network has its overall electrical input and its overall electrical output. It is designed so that its overall output will depend upon the overall input in a desired fashion; but the relationship between input and output will be far more complicated for the network as a whole than it is for any one basic unit. For example, in a computer that does addition, the network will be designed so that when there are electrical inputs corresponding to two numbers, the electrical output will correspond to the number that is the sum of these two numbers (this output can then light up a display panel to show the answer).

In very early computers, the basic units contained electric relays actual switches, opened or closed by electromagnets. Because the units were bulky and expensive, consumed considerable power, and were slow and unreliable, networks composed of them could not be very complicated. Then vacuum tubes came to be used, and later, transistors. In recent decades printed circuits have been devised where many basic units can be put on a single small wafer of material such as silicon. By making the basic units increasingly small, inexpensive, economical of power, and quick in their operations, it has become practical to devise more and more intricate networks which can adjust outputs to inputs in very complicated ways.

In thinking about a network of this kind, let us suppose that only two different voltages can occur at points in it. If we are using a 9-volt battery as our power supply, then these can be +9 volts and 0 volts; each point in the network will be at one or the other of these two voltage levels. Let us consider now some representative types of basic units of which our network may be composed.

2. Suppose we have a unit with one input point and one output point, whose operation is shown in the following table:

Input	Output
+	0
0	+

That is, the unit is constructed so that whenever its input voltage is positive, its output voltage will be zero; and whenever its input voltage is zero, its output voltage will be positive. Let us call this type of unit an "N" unit, because of its analogy with negation.

3. Next let us consider basic units having two inputs and one output each. One such unit would operate like this:

Input I	Input 2	Output
0	+	0
+	0	0
0	0	0

That is, the output is always zero except when both inputs are positive. Let us call this type of unit a "C" unit, because of its analogy with conjunction.

4. Another type of basic unit would function like this:

Input I	Input 2	Output
0	+	+
+	0	+
0	0	0

That is, the output is always positive except when both inputs are negative. Let us call this type of unit a "D" unit, because of its analogy with disjunction.

There is a striking analogy between these tables and the tables we drew up for truth-functional compounds. The first table of this section has exactly the same type of pattern as negation, the second has exactly the same type of pattern as conjunction, and the third has the same type of pattern as disjunction. The difference is that instead of truth and falsity as features of sentences, here we are dealing with two different levels of voltage as features of points in electric circuits. Nevertheless, the structural analogy between truth functions and these basic computer units is exact. As a result, we can apply what we know about truth functions to answer certain kinds of questions about computer networks.

110

In order to be able to do this, we need to correlate truth-functional formulas with combinations of basic units in the network. To see how this may be done, consider this arrangement of units:

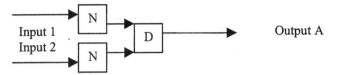

Here we may think of the inputs as corresponding to two sentence letters, say, "p" and "q"; and we may write the formula "~~p v ~q" to correspond to the whole pattern of the circuitry— the whole circuit is analogous to the disjunction of two negations. The truth or falsity of the compound formula depends in a certain way upon the truth or falsity of its component sentences; analogously, in the circuit, whether the voltage at the output is positive or zero depends in a certain way upon the voltages at the inputs. The pattern of dependence has exactly the same structure in both the logical formula and the electric circuit.

5. As another example, consider the circuit:

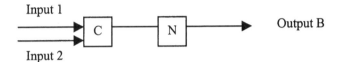

We may think of this circuit as corresponding to the formula "~(p & q)." In this circuit the output voltage again depends on the input voltages, but the circuit is not built in the same way or of the same basic units as was the previous circuit.

6. However, the question may arise: Are these two circuits equivalent in their functioning? That is, considering every possible situation, will there be the same pattern of relationship between inputs and output in both circuits? As it happens, in this case the answer is yes. If you work through the definitions, you can see that the following table is correct.

Input 1	Input 2	Output A	Output B
+	+	0	0
0	+	+	+
+	0	+	+
0	0	+	+

These two circuits are equivalent in their functioning, in that they both yield the same output for each possible combination of inputs. For us, a more direct way of detecting that these two circuits function equivalently is to notice that the formulas corresponding to them are truth-functionally equivalent, according to De Morgan's law.

In designing circuits, usually we want to avoid using any more basic units than are needed. That way, the circuit will be less expensive to build and may be more reliable in operation. Therefore, it is good to be able to recognize situations where one circuit, or portion of a circuit, can be replaced by something else more economical that will do the same job. Because of the exact analogy between switching circuits and truth functions, truth-functional symbolism can often be helpful in enabling us to tell about this. We can write down a truth-functional formula corresponding to the given circuit, and then we ask ourselves whether the formula is equivalent to some simpler truth-functional formula. If it is, then the simpler formula will indicate to us how to construct a simpler circuit.

B. Draw a diagram of a circuit composed of "N", "C", or "D" units that will perform the desired function, and write a truth-functional formula corresponding to it. In each case there are to be two inputs and one output.

1. Output is always the opposite of input 1.

2. Output is always the opposite of input 2.

3. Output is always positive.

4. Output is always zero.

5. Output is positive when and only when both inputs are positive.

6. Output is positive when and only when both inputs are zero.

7. Output is positive when and only when at least one input is positive.

8. Output is positive when and only when at least one input is zero.

9. Output is positive except when input 1 is positive and input 2 is zero.

10. Output is zero except when input 1 is positive and input 2 is zero.

11. Output is positive when and only when inputs are alike.

12. Output is positive when and only when inputs differ.

C. In each case, are the two circuits equivalent in their functioning? Make use of what you know about truth functions to establish your answers. Inputs are on the left and outputs on the right.

1.

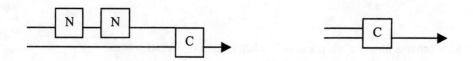

2.

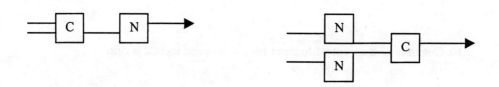

3.

4.

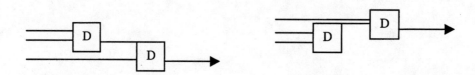

D. For each formula, draw a circuit consisting of "N", "C", and "D" units that will exhibit the same structure. Note that the number of basic letters determines the number of inputs.

1. ~p

2. p V ~p

3. p V q

4. p ⊃ q

5. q & ~q

6. p V (q & r)

7. q ≡ p

8. (q ⊃ p) & (p ⊃ q)

9. (p V q) & (q V r)

10. (p & q) ⊃ (r & s)

11. (p & r) ≡ ~ (q & r)

12. ~[p (r & s)] q

Key to Symbols and Terminology

A. Symbols:

    1. **AND** is represented in this text as either **&** or **•** and in the Manicus and Kruger text there is nothing at all representing the **AND**. So, for example, **pq** means **p & q**.

    2. **OR** is represent in this text as either **v** or **V** (the small v is used when the surrounding letters, i.e., propositions are capitalized, the large V is used when the surrounding propositions are smaller case.)

    3. **IF THEN** is represented in this text by the ⊃ alone. (Although some texts use the → sign, this is symbols means something specific in high-level logics and is not used here.)

    4. The **BICONDITIONAL** is represented in this text by the ≡ alone.

    5. The **NEGATION** sign is represented by the ~ alone. (Although some texts us the negation sign - this is not used in this text.)

    6. To represent the demarcation of the **CONCLUSION** several formats are utilized in this text:
        a. ∴ alone.
        b. / ∴
        c. _____ underneath the premises.
        d. ∴ underneath a solid line.

    7. The quantification symbol for **FOR ALL** will be found represented as either **(x)** or **(∀x)**.

    8. $(\forall x{:}Fx)Gx$ is equivalent to $(x)\,(Fx \supset Gx)$; similarly, $(\exists x{:}Fx)Gx$ is equivalent to $(\exists x)(Fx\ \&\ Gx)$.

B. Terminology:

    1. **Rules of Inference** are also know as **Rules of Deduction** or *Inferential Forms*.

    2. **Rules of Replacement** is another name for **Equivalency Rules**.

    3. **Indirect Proof Procedure** (IPP) is another name for the ***Reduction Ad Absurdum* Proof Procedure** (RAA).

Bibliography
and Permissions

Barker, Stephen F.. *The Elements of Logic.* (New York: McGraw-Hill, 1989.)
   Permissions granted by McGraw-Hill Publishing.

Churchill, Robert Paul. *Logic: An Introduction.* (New York: St. Martin's Press, Press, 1990.)
   Permissions granted by St. Martin's Press.

Gustason, William and Dolph E. Ulrich. *Elementary Symbolic Logic.* (Prospect Heights, Ill.: Waveland Press, 1973.)
   Permissions granted by Waveland Press.

Halverson, William H.. *A Concise Logic.* (New York: Random House, 1984.)
   Permissions granted by McGraw-Hill Publishing.

McKay, Thomas J.. *Modern Formal Logic.* (New York: Macmillan, 1989.)

Manicas, Peter T. and Arthur N. Kruger, *Logic: The Essentials.* (New York: Mc-Graw Hill, 1976.)
   Permissions granted by McGraw-Hill Publishing.

Neidorf, Robert. *Deductive Forms: An Elementary Logic.* (New York: Harper and Row, 1967.)
   Rights given back to author, permissions granted by Mrs. Neidorf.

Wilson, John K.. *Introductory Symbolic Logic.* (Belmont California: Wadsworth, 1992.)

Appendix

A. The below tables are for use in doing the long truth tables from Chapter Three. Feel free to copy them as many times as you need to.

B. Truth-tables for two variables:

P	Q	
T	T	
T	F	
F	T	
F	F	

C. Truth-tables for three variables:

P	Q	R	
T	T	T	
T	T	F	
T	F	T	
T	F	F	
F	T	T	
F	T	F	
F	F	T	
F	F	F	

D. For truth-tables with four variables:

P	Q	R	S	
T	T	T	T	
T	T	T	F	
T	T	F	T	
T	T	F	F	
T	F	T	T	
T	F	T	F	
T	F	F	T	
T	F	F	F	
F	T	T	T	
F	T	T	F	
F	T	F	T	
F	T	F	F	
F	F	T	T	
F	F	T	F	
F	F	F	T	
F	F	F	F	